THE PAIDEIA CLASSROOM:
TEACHING FOR UNDERSTANDING

Terry Roberts

with

Laura Billings

The National Paideia Center
University of North Carolina at Greensboro

EYE ON EDUCATION
6 DEPOT WAY WEST, SUITE 106
LARCHMONT, NY 10538
(914) 833–0551
(914) 833–0761 fax

Library of Congress Cataloging-in-Publication Data

Roberts, Terry, 1956–
    The Paideia classroom: teaching for understanding /
Terry Roberts with Laura Billings.
        p.   cm.
    Includes bibliographical references.
    ISBN 1-883001-60-9
    1. Education, Humanistic—United States.   2. Educational change—United States.   3. Education—United States—Philosophy.
I. Billings, Laura.
II. Title.
LC1011.R595   1997
370.11′2′0973—dc21   98–29063
                                                                            CIP

10 9 8 7 6 5 4 3 2

Editorial and production services provided by Richard H. Adin Freelance Editorial Services, 9 Orchard Drive, Gardiner, NY 12525 (914-883-5884)

Also Available from Eye On Education

Teaching in the Block:
Strategies for Engaging Active Learners
by Robert Lynn Canady and Michael Rettig

Performance Assessment and
Standards-based Curricula
by Allan Glatthorn
with Don Bragaw, Karen Dawkins, and John Parker

The Performance Assessment Handbook
Volume 1, Portfolios and Socratic Seminars
by Bil Johnson

The Performance Assessment Handbook
Volume 2, Performances and Exhibitions
by Bil Johnson

A Collection of Performance Tasks and Rubrics:
Upper Elementary School Mathematics
by Charlotte Danielson

A Collection of Performance Tasks and Rubrics:
Middle School Mathematics
by Charlotte Danielson

A Collection of Performance Tasks and Rubrics:
High School Mathematics
by Charlotte Danielson and Elizabeth Marquez

The Interdisciplinary Curriculum
by Arthur Ellis and Jeffrey Fouts

Research on Educational Innovations, 2d ed.
by Arthur Ellis and Jeffrey Fouts

Research on School Restructuring
by Arthur Ellis and Jeffrey Fouts

Instruction and the Learning Environment
by James Keefe and John Jenkins

The Educator's Brief Guide to the Internet
and World Wide Web
by Eugene F. Provenzo, Jr.

Teaching Mathematics in the Block
by Susan Gilkey and Carla Hunt

Teaching Foreign Languages in the Block
by Deborah Blaz

Supporting Students with Learning
Needs in the Block
by Marcia Conti-D'Antonio, Robert
Bertrando, and Joanne Eisenberger

The Reflective Supervisor
by Ray Calabrese and Sally Zepeda

Mathematics the Write Way:
Activities for Every Elementary Classroom
by Marilyn S. Neil

Data Analysis for Comprehensive
Schoolwide Improvement
by Victoria L. Bernhardt

The Directory of Innovations in Elementary Schools
by Jane McCarthy and Suzanne Still

MEET THE AUTHORS

Terry Roberts is the Executive Director of the National Paideia Center at the University of North Carolina at Greensboro. He is a former high school English teacher who, with his colleagues at the Center, works on a daily basis to improve instruction in schools across the United States. Terry Roberts is the lead author of *The Power of Paideia Schools: Defining Lives Through Learning,* published by ASCD.

Laura Billings is the Assistant Director for Curriculum and Instruction at the National Paideia Center. She is a former secondary school teacher who develops materials for Paideia instruction.

For Helen Sampson Roberts and
Margaret Billings Bauchspies

Those Who First Taught Us

TABLE OF CONTENTS

1

INTRODUCING PAIDEIA

Paideia teaching and learning is best understood as part of a comprehensive school reform program that began in 1982 with the publication of *The Paideia Proposal: An Educational Manifesto*. Written by philosopher Mortimer Adler and a network of scholars and intellectuals who called themselves the Paideia Group, this book sparked an intense debate about the quality of American public schools—a debate that gained in scope and intensity a few months later when *A Nation at Risk* was published. *The Paideia Proposal* was followed by 12 principles (see Figure 1.1) with profound implications for the classroom as well as for the entire school and community.

Although *The Paideia Proposal* gained an immediate following, it was also criticized by some teachers and principals for being so abstract that it had no practical value as a guide to building-level school reform. The Paideia Group answered this criticism by publishing *Paideia Problems and Possibilities* (1983), which was an attempt to answer the practical questions about Paideia reform that were surfacing around the country, and *The Paideia Program* (1984), which outlined in more detail the group's thoughts on the three kinds of teaching and learning that are described in it.

Because the Paideia program is one of the most comprehensive templates for whole-school reform, these books contain much information not directly related to classroom practice; they remain, however, among the best primary sources for information on Paideia teaching and learning. As several commentators have noted, Adler successfully merged two intellectual traditions: Robert Maynard Hutchins' focus on a "liberal education" with John Dewey's on active student learning. As a result, Paideia reform combines two apparently

---

FIGURE 1.1. THE PAIDEIA PRINCIPLES

- ◆ All children can learn.

- ◆ Therefore, they all deserve the same quality of schooling, not just the same quantity.

- ◆ The quality of schooling to which they are entitled is what the wisest parents would wish for their own children, the best education for the best being the best education for all.

- ◆ Schooling at its best is preparation for becoming generally educated in the course of a whole lifetime, and that schools should be judged on how well they provide such preparation.

- ◆ The three callings for which schooling should prepare all Americans are (a) to earn a decent livelihood, (b) to be a good citizen of the nation and the world, and (c) to make a good life for one's self.

- ◆ The primary cause of genuine learning is the activity of the learner's own mind, sometimes with the help of a teacher functioning as a secondary and cooperative cause.

- ◆ The three kinds of teaching that should occur in our schools are didactic teaching of subject matter, coaching that produces the skills of learning, and Socratic questioning in seminar discussion.

- ◆ The results of these three kinds of teaching should be (a) the acquisition of organized knowledge, (b) the formation of habits of skill in the use of language and mathematics, and (c) the growth of the mind's understanding of basic ideas and issues.

- ◆ Each student's achievement of these results would be evaluated in terms of that student's competencies and not solely related to the achievement of other students.

- The principal of a school should never be a mere administrator, but always a leading teacher in the school who should be cooperatively engaged with the school's teaching staff in planning, reforming, and reorganizing the school as an educational community.
- The principal and faculty of a school should themselves be actively engaged in learning.
- The desire to continue their own learning should be the prime motivation of those who dedicate their lives to the profession of teaching.

contradictory elements in American culture—intellectual standards and educational equity.

Despite this comprehensive synthesis of ideas, the Paideia program was not widely adopted as a school-reform blueprint until the early 1990s, in part because its original proponents had little actual experience in public schools and found it difficult to translate their ideals into the real world of master schedules and state-adopted texts. It took several years of implementation and experimentation in public schools to produce the final classroom model as it is presented here and the research base that is beginning to support it.

In recent years, interest in Paideia has grown dramatically, and there are now over 80 schools in 10 states that are on the way to becoming fully realized Paideia schools.

CONCEPTUAL FRAMEWORK

The Paideia program stresses a rigorous academic program for all children in the context of a whole-school program of reform. To achieve this goal, Paideia teachers strive to create a secure, caring learning environment that appeals to a wide variety of students. Within this nurturing environment, they require commitment and concentration from *all* of their students. Ultimately, the Paideia classroom should nurture both a sense of collective purpose and meaning as well as the right of each individual student to construct his or her own complex response to the world.

The Paideia classroom model features three complementary teaching techniques or "columns": didactic instruction of factual information, academic coaching of intellectual skills, and seminar discussion of values and ideas (see Figure 1.2). Adler focused on coaching and seminar leadership because didactic instruction placed the students in a fundamentally passive role. Current Paideia theory goes so far as to prescribe that a Paideia teacher should spend only 10–20% of instructional time in the didactic mode and up to 90% on techniques that produce a much larger return on the teaching investment.

Although this emphasis on active student learning is certainly not unique to Paideia, it is important to note that it is tied directly to the original 12 Paideia principles that should govern the entire school. In other words, in a fully realized Paideia school, what goes on in the classroom reflects the climate of the school that surrounds the classroom. Because both coaching and the seminar place the student in a much more active role than traditional didactic instruction, they require that the student develop intellectual self-reliance and discipline, the personal habits of mind that, in turn, foster lifelong learning.

The fully-realized Paideia classroom features units of study integrated across subject areas. In teaching these units, the Paideia teacher uses all three columns—didactic, coaching, and seminar—where appropriate, and uses them in a complementary manner. The teacher introduces students to a body of factual knowledge (didactic), coaches them in the intellectual skills necessary to manipulate and apply that knowledge (coaching), and leads them in a discussion of the ideas and values associated with that knowledge (seminar).

The original Paideia principles list three goals for the Paideia school and, within it, the Paideia classroom. The Paideia program should prepare all students to (1) earn a living successfully, (2) to participate actively in democratic self-governance, and (3) to live a life of learning. To achieve these goals, the Paideia teacher stresses the student's increasing self-reliance and self-discipline as a learner. Adler argues

FIGURE 1.2. THREE-COLUMN DIAGRAM

INSTRUCTION	COACHING	SEMINARS
Acquisition of Organized knowledge by means of **DIDACTIC INSTRUCTION** *using* Textbooks and Other Aids in the areas of: LANGUAGE LITERATURE THE FINE ARTS NATURAL SCIENCE MATHEMATICS HISTORY GEOGRAPHY and SOCIAL STUDIES	Development of Intellectual Skills by means of **COACHING** *using* Exercises and Supervised Practice in the areas of: READING WRITING CALCULATING PROBLEM-SOLVING MEASURING SPEAKING LISTENING OBSERVING and EXERCISING CRITICAL JUDGMENT	Increased Understanding of Ideas and Values by means of **SOCRATIC QUESTIONING** *using* Active Participation in the discussion of: PRIMARY SOURCE MATERIALS (Documents, Literature, NOT textbooks) WORKS OF ART INVOLVEMENT IN ARTISTIC ACTIVITIES MUSIC DRAMA and VISUAL ARTS

convincingly that a school's worth should be measured not by how its students perform on standardized tests but by how well they function as adult graduates of the school by these three measures.

Again, the two qualities that distinguish the Paideia classroom are intellectual rigor and egalitarianism. On the one hand, Adler asks that students master a core curriculum (including the arts and a foreign language) that stresses the classics,[1] and on the other hand, he stresses how important it is to democracy that all students succeed at a high level. Adler has argued for this connection between democracy and education consistently, and it is an important characteristic of the teaching techniques in a Paideia classroom. For example, the seminar stresses the ability of students to generate, articulate, and justify ideas—in other words, to think, *for themselves*. In this way, each student's ideas are valued, and every student is expected to contribute to the discussion. During the seminar, individuals learn to be more active contributors to a group dynamic, learning in microcosm how to be dynamic citizens while at the same time practicing significant intellectual skills.

Adler's emphasis on the student's eventual ability to earn a living does not mean that students should be tracked into vocational courses or magnet schools with strictly vocational themes. He is adamant about the futility of this approach to preparing students for the world of work, and recent studies on workforce preparedness support his argument (see, for example, the 1991 federal report "The Secretary's Commission on Achieving Necessary Skills"). Instead, Paideia teachers believe that all students follow the same course of rigorous study, and that a solid liberal arts education is the best preparation either for postsecondary education or entering the job market. Seen in this light, it is clear that both the seminar and coaching columns ask students to practice academic skills (communication, cooperation, problem solving) that most experts cite as the key to success in the mercurial and highly technical world of twenty-first century vocations.

---

1. It is interesting to note that E.D. Hirsch's current emphasis on "cultural literacy" and the "core knowledge" movement owe a direct debt to Adler and, beyond Adler, to Hutchins.

In this way, job preparedness is one aspect of the general theme of lifelong learning, the center piece in Paideia's goals for the school and classroom. Adler's emphasis on lifelong learning has several implications for how classrooms are managed and lessons taught. First, it is important that teachers adopt the role of lifelong learners—adults who actively pursue their own fascination with learning—and provide children with role models. Second, it is equally important that teachers help individual children develop as self-reliant, self-motivated learners who will continue to actively interact with the world long after they finish their time in school. Not only does the seminar stress the importance of each child generating and articulating his or her own ideas, the coaching column stresses student self-reliance in a broad spectrum of ways that lead to lifelong learning.

Ultimately, all three Paideia teaching columns are designed to be used in concert to produce high school graduates that are active, independent learners. The student's role in response to didactic instruction is to record and digest a body of objective or subjective information. The student then learns to manipulate and apply that information in response to the teacher's coaching. The student's application of knowledge is often done in the context of solving real-world problems and producing real-world products, working sometimes alone and sometimes as a member of a group. Finally, the student must learn to consider the abstract elements inherent to the body of knowledge while engaged in seminar discussion, dissecting the ideas and values as suggested by a relevant seminar text. Both the coaching and seminar columns are designed to wean the student of his or her dependence on the teacher for information and guidance, ultimately creating the sort of intellectual independence that characterizes the lifelong learner.

CLASSROOM ORGANIZATION

The first of the three columns, didactic instruction, is focused on teaching students facts, concepts, information, and formulas through texts, lectures, demonstrations, and a wide range of audiovisual material (see Figure 1.2, p. 7). Ideally, didactic instruction is extremely efficient, introducing the core of a body of knowledge in a coherent, well-organized fashion. Because this type of instruction places the student in such a passive role, however, the best teachers have long practiced making even didactic instruction as interactive as possible, asking numerous questions of students and encouraging them to introduce questions. The goal of didactic instruction is to provide students with a body of information that they can then apply and manipulate in the other two columns.

Within the context of well-coached projects, students can learn to control, manipulate, and apply that information within a relevant framework. In *The Paideia Program*, Adler and Sizer describe coaching in some detail, but the resulting definition suggests one-on-one or small-group tutorials that are simply impossible for most classroom teachers to schedule. As a result, several Paideia schools have drastically altered their schedules or created special "labs" to produce the small teacher-to-student ratio necessary for this type of coaching. More recently, successful Paideia teachers have learned to combine a wide variety of cooperative learning techniques with the product-oriented project to create the special coaching program described here. The reason for this focus on product-oriented projects is that this context makes the work being done in school much more relevant to *students*, which, in turn, leads to more focused, intense student work and to more durable and detailed learning.

If the goal of didactic instruction is to provide students with a body of knowledge, then the goal of the coached project is to put students in the position of having to manipulate and apply that knowledge in a context that is relevant to them personally (Figure 1.2, p. 7). One example of this is the high school class which, during a year of social studies dedicated to state history, became involved in the restoration of the oldest building in their county and created a small book of photos and text to record the reconstruction. This, in turn, led to plans for the following year's classes to begin the process of turning the restored building into a county museum to be staffed in part by high school students who were using their internships there to satisfy the school's community service requirement. All of these projects involved many hours of well-coached academic work that students gladly participated in because they easily understood the relevance of what they were doing.

If the goal of the first two columns is to introduce students to a body of knowledge and help them learn to manipulate and apply that knowledge, then the goal of the seminar is to have them learn to think abstractly and communicate clearly about ideas (Figure 1.2, p. 7). This takes them beyond the practical application side of academic skills and into the higher order thinking side. Because this is typically done by focusing on a classical text that addresses relevant ideas or values, students are also exposed to what people of other ages and cultures have thought and felt about the same body of knowledge and its implications.

Many teachers have been exposed to only one or two of the three columns and so don't apply them in a rigorous and complementary plan. Obviously, all three columns work best when applied in concert—both because they are designed to accomplish quite different learning goals and because students of varied learning styles respond differently to the three columns. To engage as large a percentage of any class group as possible, a wise teacher uses all three types of teaching and learning in an effective cycle. Figure 1.3 (see next page) lists the essential elements of a Paideia classroom.

FIGURE 1.3. ESSENTIAL ELEMENTS OF A PAIDEIA CLASSROOM

1. A Paideia classroom is a student-centered classroom.

   Goals

   ♦ Increased student pride in their work
   ♦ Greater involvement and interaction by teacher, students, and the community
   ♦ Increased student responsibility for their own learning

2. A Paideia classroom is dedicated to the learning of *all* students.

   Goals

   ♦ Cooperative learning
   ♦ Family involvement and advocacy
   ♦ Classroom-community partnerships
   ♦ Extended school campus
   ♦ Reciprocity of service and resources between classroom and community

3. The Paideia teacher uses Paideia seminars as a central teaching/learning device.

   Goals

   ♦ Chairs in a circle
   ♦ Art, music, primary sources
   ♦ Rich in printed material
   ♦ Art of conversation in evidence
   ♦ Civil disagreements

4. The Paideia teacher uses coached project learning for the majority of the instructional program.

   Goals

   ♦ Students planning
   ♦ Students designing
   ♦ Students working

- ◆ Students evaluating
- ◆ Students producing

5. The Paideia teacher uses relatively little didactic instruction and that which the teacher does use is of very high quality.

   Goals

   - ◆ Excellent lecturing
   - ◆ Limited lecturing
   - ◆ Higher-order thinking interaction as a part of lecturing
   - ◆ Quality, creative audiovisuals and demonstrations

6. In a Paideia classroom, assessment of students and teacher is individualized rather than standardized —emphasizing individual growth.

   Goals

   - ◆ Student and teacher exhibitions and publications
   - ◆ Students and teacher planning and designing together
   - ◆ Open communication about classroom policy and curriculum
   - ◆ Student responsibility for learning
   - ◆ Teacher evaluation that reflects Paideia strategies as goals

7. A Paideia classroom is dedicated to the intellectual development of both children and adults.

   Goals

   - ◆ Lifelong learning
   - ◆ Rigorous curriculum
   - ◆ Reading, writing, discussion
   - ◆ Classics in the classroom
   - ◆ High expectations for students and teacher

8. The Paideia teacher is a model lifelong learner.

Goals

- Teacher as generalist
- Teacher reading and discussing what the teacher reads with students
- High quality teacher exhibits and projects

9. A Paideia classroom is part of a larger (school) community dedicated to lifelong learning.

Goals

- Faculty seminars
- Community seminars
- Parents and other community members involved in coached projects
- Use of school resources to enhance community learning

2

DIDACTIC INSTRUCTION

Adler's humorous description of the traditional lecture is the transfer of information from the notes of the lecturer to the notes of the audience without that information passing through the minds of either. Well-trained didactic presenters focus their efforts on making sure the information they present passes through the minds of the students on the way to being recorded in their notes. This often means using a wide variety of didactic techniques within the same presentation. It also means that most effective didactic lessons are short, dramatic, and dense with vital information. In a well-planned unit of study, didactic presentation should probably not exceed 10–15% of class time.

THE TEACHER

During a didactic lesson the teacher takes on the role of the expert who is dispensing essential knowledge. To be able to perform this role effectively, the teacher needs to prepare as follows:

- Identify what is the "must know" core of information from the lesson plan and organize it clearly;
- Identify the desired results of the lesson in terms of student knowledge and skill;
- Prepare a variety of didactic techniques (lecture, reading material, handouts, audiovisual aids, demonstration and/or performance elements) to be used together or in sequence;
- Plan how students will be led to interact both with the presenter and with the material;

- Prepare any materials that will be presented and/or placed in the hands of the students;
- Study the information sufficiently enough so as not to be tied to a set of notes at a podium or desk while presenting.

All of these suggestions assume that a teacher is preparing for a dynamic, even dramatic, presentation, not a boring lecture read directly from a set of notes or overhead transparencies.

Truly talented presenters tend to have a number of things in common. They are enthusiastic about their audience and the material under discussion. They are dynamic, often moving around the room while they speak and involving the audience by asking and answering questions in order to highlight key points. They are organized—their presentations have both an identified structure and a clear goal—without being slavishly attached to their outlines. They use the full resources of their voices and body language to engage and hold the audience's attention. The ability to produce memorable didactic lessons is more like an actor assuming a role than it is the dramatic posturing of an extroverted personality—it is a set of skills to be learned and practiced.

THE CLASSROOM

The traditional classroom arrangement of student chairs in straight rows facing the front of the room and the teacher's desk or podium is a poor design even for didactic instruction. Straight rows block the direct lines of sight and hearing that are crucial for good didactic teaching, and they banish certain students to the back of the classroom as far as possible from the action. When arranging a classroom for a lecture, audiovisual presentation, or demonstration, a wise teacher takes his or her lead from the best designed churches, theaters, and stadiums.

The first rule for didactic classroom arrangement is to take the maximum number of students expected and arrange their seats so that they can all be placed as close to the presentation point as possible while maintaining clear sight lines and freedom of movement for the presenter. At times a lab table or audiovisual equipment will dictate class arrangement, but when the presenter is the only point of interest, a circle or semicircle that brings students closer to the presenter is in order.

The second rule is that the presenter needs to be able to move freely around the room so that the presenter is able to stand beside a sleepy or disruptive student or group while continuing to lecture or direct the discussion. There is a dramatic difference from the students' point of view in listening to a lecture from a stationary speaker who is tied to his or her notes and listening to a presentation from a mobile, enthusiastic presenter who moves about the room from place to place: demonstrating, questioning, explaining, and illustrating.

The common factor in both these rules is reducing the physical and cognitive distance between presenter and audience so that students assume a much more active role in interacting both with the speaker and the material.

If the goal of a didactic session is to convey a coherent body of factual knowledge in as efficient a manner as possible, then the presenter should use visual and aural aids, handouts, demonstrations, and discussion to enhance a lecture, not lengthen or diffuse it. For example, one videotaped scene from *Hamlet* illuminates a discussion of blank verse while seeing the entire play buries it. A handout that outlines the information in a lecture through a series of questions (leaving space on the sheet for the students to fill in the answers and ask their own questions in turn) guides the students in their note-taking without giving all the information away. The best didactic lessons are short and to the point.

Typically, a good didactic teacher outlines the material to be presented on a handout or on the chalk board prior to the lesson itself so that the students can anticipate where the presentation is going and how the presenter intends to take them there. The presenter should briefly go over this outline and stress what the students should know and/or be able to do after the presentation (even if it is very short). This quick overview gives the students a learning "target" so that at the end of the lesson they are capable of judging their own progress relative to the goal.

While the primary didactic teaching tool is the lecture, good lecturers enhance their voice with visual or aural aids, with demonstrations of skills or processes, and with hand-outs that guide the students' participation with the material. These enhancements include common tools such as the chalkboard, overhead projector, video or keyboard projections, problem-solving or lab demonstrations, and handouts that guide the students' note-taking. Several of these materials can be used to enhance any basic lecture presentation, particularly as they encourage active discussion between students and between the students and presenter. Discussion is the natural outgrowth of a strong didactic presentation, and it should be encouraged up to a point. When discussion distracts students from the topic at hand or lengthens the lesson to the point where students begin to lose interest, the teacher can pull the students back to the original topic.

When planning and presenting didactic lessons, remember that efficient presentation of a coherent set of information is the goal. "Efficient presentation" means more than *brief*; it also means that students are intently engaged with both presenter and material so that they comprehend and digest the information in question.

3

ACADEMIC
COACHING

Coaching has proven to be the most difficult of the three Paideia columns to apply in the classroom for several reasons. First, Adler and Sizer originally described coaching as if it could only occur in a tutorial or small group situation (see *Paideia Program*, pp. 32–46). This restriction complicated implementation for the average public school teacher, faced with a class size of anywhere from 20 to 35. In addition, the original description did little to formalize coaching in the same way that it formalized the seminar as a teaching technique, and this, too, led to some doubt and disagreement about whether coaching was actually very different from the types of guided practice or cooperative learning used across the country. As it is defined here, academic coaching draws on the original definition of Adler and Sizer but takes the concept to a much more formal level where it is possible for teachers to be effectively trained, tactfully coached, and eventually attain mastery as coaches.

This new, more sophisticated definition of coaching focuses on the teacher-student relationship within a formal product-oriented classroom project. It should be noted here that the coached classroom project owes as much to the classroom practices of "Foxfire," expeditionary learning, and cooperative learning theories, as it does to Adler and Sizer's original description. In other words, it draws on a number of complementary trends in current pedagogical theory in order to create a second column that has as dramatic an impact on the learning lives of students as does the Paideia seminar.

In addition, it is important to remember that because coaching occupies 60–80% of instructional time in a Paideia classroom, the product-oriented project often becomes the organizing principle for all three columns.

It helps to think of coaching as the kinds of facilitation of student work that occur as students participate in projects singly or in groups, wherein they are "coached" by their teachers, by each other, and by outside experts. The ultimate, defining characteristic of these academic projects is that they culminate in a product of real-world value, thus motivating students to practice intently the skills involved in producing the product.

Ideally, *project* in this instance means that teachers are asking students to produce a quality product that involves several academic disciplines and most or all of Gardner's eight intelligences.[1] The duration of the project is usually that of a traditional unit of study. The product is significant enough to have value in the world outside the classroom, often as sophisticated as a dramatic production, a student-built structure, or a book.

As always in the Paideia classroom, students are coached in heterogeneous groups and each group is held accountable by itself and the coach for the quality of its product. The accountability is performance-based and noncompetitive. Within this framework, individual student achievement can be evaluated according to individual progress rather than standardized measures. (Checklists and rubrics leading to portfolios combined with narrative evaluations are a natural complement to the coaching process.)

The most instructive way to think about the quality of the coached process is not in terms of what the teacher does, but rather in terms of what the students experience. That is why the 12 Principles of Intellectual Coaching (see Figure 3.1) are written specifically from the student's point of view.

---

1. In his 1985 book *Frames of Mind,* Howard Gardner described seven intelligences that have come to define lesson planning and teaching that engages students through their multiple intelligences. He has since added an eighth "intelligence": the *naturalistic.*

FIGURE 3.1. PRINCIPLES OF INTELLECTUAL COACHING

The coached process is more intense, more lasting, and more meaningful the more that:

- Students discover and construct their own meaning out of the project in a personally significant way. (This can mean helping to design the assignment as well as the ways in which they will be evaluated.)

- Students exercise their own power of choice in an increasingly responsible and mature way.

- Students build on the past and anticipate the future—their own and that of others.

- The individual student defines himself or herself through the process, both interpersonally and intrapersonally.

- The individual student validates his or her sense of control and competence as expectations of success are confirmed and challenged.

- The various tasks that are part of the process are relevant to the individual students and have obvious value in the world outside the classroom.

- The various tasks involved in the process are both challenging and novel.

- Students are not motivated by negative cognition or emotions—including almost all those associated with traditional, competitive grading.

- Students successfully communicate and cooperate with a wide variety of others in a wide variety of settings.

- Individual students treat each other with respect and courtesy, stressing that each has unique and valuable talents.

- ◆ Cultural and environmental differences among individual students and among those others associated with the project are not only accepted—they are valued.

- ◆ Students periodically review the process and assess how and what they are, and are not, learning.

THE TEACHER

The role of the teacher in the coaching column is like that of the master craftsman at work surrounded by apprentices. The master craftsman is a recognized expert in the process at hand and is actively involved with the apprentices in the creation of the product for which the shop exists. In this role, the teacher works *with* students, helping them perfect their skills so that the end product of their common labor is of the highest quality.

Consider, for example, a group of middle school students studying American history. As part of their study of 20th century American culture, they are staging a production of *Inherit the Wind*, a 1955 drama based on the Scopes "monkey trial" in which a young science teacher was tried and convicted of teaching evolution. The teacher acts as the director of the play; the preparations (including a seminar on the text; see Chapter 4) and rehearsals make up the coached "process"; and the production itself is the product. The teacher, like any drama director, takes on many roles during the period of time between the first read-through and closing night, but ultimately the teacher's job is to bring out the best work possible from every student involved in each aspect of the production.

The most common role of the teacher during a coached project occurs when the teacher interacts directly with a student or group of students at work. The teacher responds to questions, models effective skills, offers suggestions, and asks questions—all intended to guide student practice. Figure 3.2 is a handy reference to asking thought-provoking questions; teachers can use this guide or one like it to use their own questioning techniques as they move from one group to another.

FIGURE 3.2. COACHING INTELLECTUAL SKILLS

Within the framework of the ongoing coached project, teachers should find ample opportunity to coach the intellectual skills of the students. Teachers should respect the range and depth of student thought by consistently challenging them:

Use of Precise Terminology

Instead of saying:	*Say:*
"Let's look at these two pictures."	"Let's compare these two pictures."
"What do you think will happen when…?"	"What do you predict will happen when…?"
"How can you put into groups…?"	"How can you classify…?"
"Let's work this problem."	"Let's analyze this problem."
"How do you know that's true?"	"What evidence can you find…?"

Provide Data, Not Solutions

- Encourage autonomy
- Supply varied stimuli—visual, auditory, numeric, melodic, etc.

Give Direction

- Require students to analyze a task, identify what is needed for completion

Probe for Specificity—Question

- Universals
- Comparisons
- Unreferenced pronouns
- Unspecified groups
- Assumed rules or traditions

Encourage Metacognition
- Thinking about thinking

Analyze the Logic of Language
- Describe steps taken to arrive at answers
- Determine a plan of action

THE STUDENT

If the most telling analogy for the teacher-coach is that of master craftsman, then the best analogy for the role of the student is that of apprentice to master. The apprentice works closely with the master, either alone or with other apprentices, learning by doing all the tasks that are involved in producing the product. The skill level of the apprentice may fall anywhere across a broad spectrum from novice to near mastery, but the defining element of effective apprenticeship is that the apprentice is constantly improving. No apprentice can gain mastery by learning only a few of the many jobs involved in producing the shop's best work; rather, the apprentice must learn a large number of interrelated tasks in order to assure the quality of the work.

To return to the example of the cast and crew of *Inherit the Wind*, every student in that middle school team will play a key role in creating the highest quality production possible—those involved in set design and construction, costuming, makeup, and script editing, as well as those who actually perform the roles. Students will find it necessary to stay focused while working alone, and they will have to work closely with groups of other students and adults. The intellectual skills involved that are specific to language arts alone include reading, writing, speaking, listening, and thinking—the entire gamut of the liberal arts. Most importantly, the fact of the production itself gives the intense work involved meaning for the students.

FIGURE 3.3. COACHED PROJECT CHECKLIST

These questions are designed for teachers and students to use together in planning and implementing a coached project in their classroom. They are intended to be used under the supervision of teachers who have been trained by the staff of the National Paideia Center and as an "assessment" tool. In other words, the checklist cannot be used to evaluate teachers or to assign individual students a grade, but rather to help both teachers and students learn and work more powerfully together.

Questions to Ask When Planning a Project

1. Does the project address a "real world" problem?

2. Does the problem have meaning for the majority of students in the classroom?

3. Is there a real audience for the project work?

4. Will the project ask students to apply knowledge and skills prescribed for at least one discipline or content area?

5. Are students actively involved in designing the project?

6. Are students actively involved in defining the end product of the project?

7. Are students actively involved in projecting quality control criteria for the product?

8. Will a variety of adults from outside the classroom be involved in the project?

9. Will a variety of adults from outside the classroom be involved in the assessment of the end product?

Questions to Ask Periodically During the Project

10. Is the classroom furniture and equipment arranged to facilitate the production of the product?

11. Are there well-organized work stations in the classroom dedicated to the production of various elements of the product?

12. Is a prototype of the finished product displayed (or readily available to teacher and students) in the room?

13. Is a work calendar of events and deadlines leading up to the target date for the finished product displayed in the room?

14. Are a variety of adults with relevant expertise and experience available to model for and coach student work?

15. Do teacher and students spend significant amounts of time doing field-based work on the project?

16. Do teacher and students engage in real investigation and research, using a variety of methods, media, and sources in their exploration?

17. Do teacher and students together exercise skills in a wide range of intellectual skills?

18. Do teacher and students regularly engage in detailed and candid assessment, both of their progress and of the eventual product? (As they move closer to the end of the project, they may find it necessary to redesign the final product.)

19. Do teacher and students use a variety of methods and media (including the appropriate technologies) in the actual creation of the final product?

20. Is seminar discussion of a relevant text or texts included in the ongoing project?

Questions to Ask When the Project is Completed

21. Is the final product evaluated by real world criteria and by a variety of experienced adults?

22. Is the final product formally presented to its real world audience by teacher and students working in concert?

23. Do teacher and students engage in a reflective assessment of their work together over the course of the project?

24. Do teacher and students engage in a comprehensive self-assessment as individuals involved in the project?

25. Is a final "grade" for each student negotiated through a balance of adult, peer, and self-assessment?

THE CLASSROOM

The physical setting of a coaching classroom is determined by the product in production. To get a good idea of what this might mean, visit a local high school and examine these rooms:

♦ Any traditional shop or vocational classroom—carpentry, masonry, agriculture, mechanics, nursing—where students are learning skills specific to a "trade."

♦ The drama, choral, or instrumental music room where students are preparing for a performance.

♦ The journalism or annual staff room where students are preparing this year's annual or the next issue of the school paper.

♦ The art room where students are preparing an exhibition of student work.

The common factors that unite these spaces are the involvement of students in active learning by doing and the sense of quality control imposed by having to produce a product of real worth. Ultimately, there can be no one way to design a classroom to be used for academic coaching; the classroom has to be organized according to the project currently under way—play rehearsal, book production, historical simulation, or science experiments.

For years vocational teachers have altered the traditional high school schedule to take students off-campus to "live project" sites where they were actively involved in building homes, repairing school property, or performing community service projects. These courses had an impact in contemporary school reform with movements such as expeditionary learning, service learning, and schools without walls. Ultimately, teachers who become expert in coaching intellectual skills discover that not only must their individual classrooms be very fluid in design but that it is often necessary to go beyond the physical setting of the classroom itself to obtain the highest quality work.

REAL PRODUCTS FOR REAL AUDIENCES

Teachers and students engaged in planning a coached project often find it valuable to consult a list of possible products to prime their imaginations. Obviously, no such list will ever be complete, but Figure 3.4, on pages 34–35, is a good one because it's organized into types and it contains a wide variety of items.

Each of the entries in the list should also suggest a spectrum of applications. For example, the first item, an advertisement, suddenly takes on new meaning when teachers realize they can advertise a wide variety of elements of their course or school. They can advertise events, contests, productions, publications, demonstrations, and.... The list is all but endless.

Imagine for a moment two middle schools being consolidated into one in order to move into a new building. The building is large and complex, with several wings and "pods" of classrooms. One team produces a campus map drawn to scale and color-coded to key which team occupies which sections of the building. The math, art, and technology applications of the project are obvious, but teachers are surprised when the "rough draft" field-text reveals the need for an explanatory narrative on the reverse side of the map. At that point, it becomes a language arts project as well.

During the early stages of the project, both teachers and students forgot to consider the map's audiences. After the first draft, teachers and students used the list in Figure 3.5 to predict that new students and their families, as well as first-time visitors to the campus, would need the map. When they placed copies of a second draft of the map in the front office along with requests for feedback, they discovered that the number of non-English speaking new students (and their families) dictated Spanish as well as English labels and narrative on the map. Furthermore, the number of visitors to the school was increasing so dramatically that the office staff requested a second map showing the location of the school campus and giving clear directions to the school from three major highways. The audiences for one map led directly to a product revision and to a second project.

FIGURE 3.4. COACHED PRODUCTS AND PERFORMANCES

Key Question: What student product(s) and/or performance(s) will provide evidence of proficiency related to the identified outcome(s) or standard(s)?
Student products and performances should be guided by a **purpose** and an **audience**.

Written Products	Oral Products	Visual Products	Other Products
Advertisement	Audiotape	Banner	Environmental project
Biography	Debate	Cartoon	Mural
Book report review	Discussion	Collage	Quilt
Brochure	Dramatization	Collection	Renovation of historical site
Crossword puzzle	Interview	Computer graphic	Textbook
Editorial	Newscast	Construction	Water testing kit
Essay	Oral presentation	Data table	
Experiment record	Oral report	Design	
Game	Play	Diagram	
Journal	Poetry reading	Display	
Lab report	Rap	Diorama	
Letter	Skit	Drawing	

Written Products	Oral Products	Visual Products	Other Products
Log	Song	Filmstrip	
Magazine article	Teach a lesson	Graph	
Memo	Readers' theater	Map	
Newspaper article		Model	
Poem		Painting	
Proposal		Photograph	
Questionnaire		Poster	
Research report		Scrapbook	
Script		Sculpture	
		Slide show	
		Storyboard	
		Videotape	

FIGURE 3.5. AUDIENCES FOR PRODUCTS AND PERFORMANCES

- Advertisers
- Board members (school, community, foundations,...)
- Bosses
- Business/corporations—local, regional, national
- Celebrities—entertainers, musicians, athletes, TV/movie stars
- Community member/helps
- Customers/consumers
- Experts/expert panels
- Family members (parents, grandparents, siblings, etc.)
- Fellow/younger/older students
- Foreign embassy staff
- Friends
- Government/elected officials
- Historical figures
- Judges
- Jury
- Museum visitors
- Neighbors
- Other school staff (principal, counselor, secretary)
- Pen pals
- Radio listeners
- Readers—newspaper, magazine, etc.
- Relatives
- Teachers
- Television viewers
- Travel agents
- Travelers
- Visitors (to school, community)

Of the three Paideia columns, coaching is the teaching and learning construct that breaks down most of the traditional school barriers that limit learning. For example, to run the kind of coached unit suggested here requires flexibility in terms of time (longer units of time for focused student labor), space (taking students to "live" academic projects), materials (the raw material of production), role of the teacher (outside experts and other students coaching students), and role of the student (planner, designer, worker, quality control engineer).

If the first Paideia column, didactic instruction, is designed to relay factual knowledge, then the second column, coaching, is designed to allow students to manipulate and apply that knowledge. When students manipulate and apply knowledge, they master both the knowledge base itself and the skillful self-reliance that leads directly to lifelong learning.

4

THE PAIDEIA
SEMINAR

Unlike coaching, the seminar has been a clearly, even formally, defined teaching technique since the beginning of Paideia reform. It is a formal discussion based on a text in which the leader asks only open-ended questions. Within the context of the discussion, students are required to read and study the text carefully, listen closely to the comments of others, think critically for themselves, and articulate both their own thoughts and their responses to the thoughts of others. In other words, every seminar in which students participate hones their language skills. In the seminar, unlike in the coaching paradigm, students are also sharpening their skills in applying abstractions—ideas and values.

The seminar is in many ways the culmination of the Paideia learning experience. It is in the seminar circle that students examine the ideas and values inherent in the body of knowledge to which they were introduced didactically and which they learned to apply in coached project work. They engage routinely in higher-order thinking because to participate in a seminar they must summarize, analyze, synthesize, compare, and contrast, logically defending and challenging their own ideas and those of others.

In essence, the seminar is designed to place students in the position of having to think critically for themselves so that they develop the ability to:

♦ Discuss and understand ideas and values

♦ Solve abstract problems

♦ Make more mature and more sophisticated decisions

♦ Resolve conflicts between people and ideas

◆ Apply knowledge and skills (learned in didactic and coached lessons) to new situations

◆ Value discussion as a means of learning

◆ Value classical works of art, the social sciences, and literature springboards to learning

Ultimately, seminar skills—critical thinking, willingness to address abstract ideas and values, and the ability to listen and articulate coherently—should become deeply ingrained habits of both teacher and student alike, learning behaviors that characterize every moment of classroom life.

To achieve these intellectual skills as a "product," it is imperative that both teachers and students understand the "process" of a powerful discussion. A successful seminar honors both the community of discussion and the individual within that community. It generates a synergy of ideas by freeing genuine discussion, by empowering diversity, and by creating shared intellectual experience. The words *communication* and *community* stem from the same Latin root: *communis* or common. A seminar can only succeed if the individual member of the group is free to express his or her thoughts openly and without fear of reprisal. For this reason, it is extremely important that teachers clearly define and consistently coach the behaviors that contribute to respectful dialogue. The result is the richest mix of ideas possible in any classroom because the ideas flow directly from the students and because all students are included.

THE TEACHER

The role of the teacher during the Paideia seminar itself can appear to be quite passive; basically the teacher facilitates a discussion among the student participants, asking evocative questions but otherwise staying out of the way. Experienced seminar leaders will testify, however, that quality leadership is much more complicated than it often appears, and the most difficult part may be the preparation that leads to a successful seminar.

Preparing to lead a Paideia seminar involves everything from selecting a text to coaching the participants in active reading and respectful discourse; and from writing good Socratic questions to anticipating and preparing for possible responses. Preparation can sometimes be both difficult and time-consuming, but it is the key to a successful seminar.

Increasingly, experienced seminar leaders emphasize the importance of assigning preseminar activities that ensure students have read the text closely, have taken detailed notes, and have otherwise prepared for a discussion. Some preseminar activities are best completed outside class (research, for example), while some are best coached by the teacher; some are best completed independently (writing a formal opening statement in response to a specific question), while others are best addressed collaboratively (close reading of the "surface" meaning of the text). Because the seminar is intended to be about the ideas and concepts embedded in a text, not the factual information, the quality of the discussion often depends on students having dealt with issues of basic reading comprehension before the seminar ever starts.

LINEAR INEQUALITIES: A SEMINAR INTEGRATED INTO ALGEBRA I

Math teachers often complain that students fail to remember the concepts they have been taught from one chapter or unit to another, and to transfer key concepts from one problem to another. Recent studies of how American teachers teach math suggest students need less repetitious drill and practice and more opportunity to discuss concepts and practice multiple strategies for solving a problem.

A seminar on a math problem from the chapter or unit in question is an excellent way to provide students with the opportunity to do both. For example, one high school Algebra I teacher now makes a practice of introducing the chapter on "linear inequalities" by holding a seminar on this problem:

> Maria and Joe are on the same swim team. Maria lives five miles from the pool where they practice; Joe lives three miles from the pool. How far apart do Maria and Joe live?

The opening question asked students in pairs to articulate how they would solve the problem, and the leader focused the discussion on describing as many different strategies as possible. Core questions asked students to consider different possibilities for where the two swimmers might live in relation to each other. At some point during the seminar, students were able to describe clearly the range of right answers, but the teacher asked them to continue to explore different ways of solving the problem.

Over the next few days of class, the teacher used didactic presentation and skills practice to help students apply the concept of linear inequalities in solving a variety of problems.

Basically, a successful leader prepares the proper environment for student discussion, prepares the students to participate in such a discussion, and then, if all goes well, plays a deceptively passive role during the seminar itself (see Fig. 4.1). Once a seminar among practiced participants begins, seemingly the teacher's only job is to ask questions and, even more to the point, open-ended questions that don't force the students into the teacher's premeditated conclusions. To facilitate a quality discussion involving all the participants, however, a good seminar leader must keep track of a number of different threads in the conversation, record in some way who is and is not talking, remain conscious of the text as the anchor of the discussion, and respond appropriately when obviously erroneous information is introduced by a participant. Many leaders learn to manage all these different aspects of the discussion by taking notes (often on a seating chart so they can sort them at a glance) during the discussion.

The most common problem faced by inexperienced seminar leaders is how to bring shy or uninvolved students into the conversation and how to keep aggressive students from dominating. Part of seminar training for teachers involves a range of tactics for both types of student, the use of which often depends on why and how a participant avoids or dominates the discussion. Another adjustment that active classroom teachers find difficult to make is not controlling the discussion, thereby allowing students to work out their own answers to questions without input from the authority figure. It is very important that they do so, however, because the ultimate function of the seminar is to wean the students of leaning on their teacher anytime complex and/or abstract issues surface. This prepares them for dealing with complex and abstract learning problems as they become adults.

FIGURE 4.1. WRITING SEMINAR QUESTIONS

When first learning to lead seminars, teachers often find it useful to prepare three kinds of questions: opening, core, and closing.

Opening questions are usually the most open-ended of the three types and are often designed to elicit the ideas embedded in a text that are the most evocative for the participants. Examples include:

- Another (better) title for this piece would be _____?
- The most important word in this piece is _____?
- The most important sentence (passage) is _____?
- The central conflict in this piece is _____?
- Based on this text, would you say the author would agree or disagree with this statement: _____?

Questions for a Paideia seminar should:

- Always be open-ended (have more than one right answer);
- Analyze the essential ideas in the text (including those ideas that seem most important to the participants);
- Examine ideas, concepts, and values (not facts);
- If it is a yes/no question, introduce a planned follow-up question; and
- Focus participants attention on the text or on their relationship to the text.

Core questions are often the least open-ended of the three types. Core questions ask participants to examine specific ideas that have come up in discussion or specific passages in the text. Often, core questions flow directly out of participant comments. Examples include:

- What is meant by (a specific quote)?
- Why do you say that? *or* Explain what you mean by _____.
- Tell me more about (your last comment)....
- What do you mean by that word (phrase, or comment)?
- Where do you find support for that in the text?
- Is it contradictory to state _____ in one part of the text and _____ in another?
- In what ways are _____ and _____ alike and/or different?
- Do the rest of you agree or disagree with (name of participant)? Why?

Closing Questions usually ask participants to focus on how the ideas in the text relate to their own lives or to meditate on how their thinking evolved during the course of the seminar. Examples include:

- If you were (the character) in this piece, what would you say or do?
- What does this text teach us about (issue of particular importance to participants)?
- Re-ask the opening question and examine why participants changed their minds.
- What did you learn during this discussion? What prompted your learning?

Just as preseminar activities often contribute to the quality of the discussion itself, postseminar activities capitalize on the learning that takes place there. Because the seminar itself demands close and critical reading, speaking, listening, and thinking, many leaders focus on the writing process as a powerful complement to the seminar—one that causes students to develop their ideas even further and in a way that makes them even more memorable. Most experienced leaders focus on the participants' actual seminar skills (process) as well as their mastery of the concepts (content), so that subsequent seminars will be of higher and higher quality (see Appendix C).

The best seminars are actually a three-stage process: preseminar activities that prepare students for quality participation, the discussion itself, and postseminar activities that maximize the learning of both the group and the individuals within that group. The best seminar leaders master all three stages.

Although schools often begin seminar practice with schoolwide seminar programs that ask all teachers to practice the process with their classes on the same day if not at the same hour, the goal is for each teacher to fully integrate seminars into the learning life of his or her individual classroom. Figures 4.2 and 4.3 are excerpts from two lesson-plan books: one, a second grade unit on "weather," and the other, a secondary social studies unit on the Constitution. In both instances, there are several possible seminar texts suggested, and the resourceful teacher will discover even more as he or she teaches the curriculum in question. It is also worth noting that seminars early in a unit arouse student interest and generate questions that can focus the unit on student concerns. Seminars late in a unit can serve as capstone activities, where students use what they've learned to generate ideas of their own about the topic. Paideia teachers will often use two or three seminars to fully access the conceptual content of a unit of study.

FIGURE 4.2. INTEGRATING SEMINARS:
SECOND GRADE SCIENCE

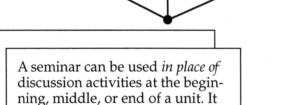

♦ Read *Weather World* by Gail Gibbons
♦ Create display chart with vocabulary words
♦ Lead discussion of water cycle (poster)
	♦ Make rain using experiment in *Copycat*
	♦ Begin project
	  • Students assigned to groups
	  • Students to begin puzzle activity; assign roles
	  • Distribute outline and rubric for project
		♦ Do experiment "Water, Water Everywhere"
		♦ Students work in pairs (using book) to design a specific weather pattern
		♦ *Homework*: begin reading *Thunder Cake*

A seminar can be used *in place of* discussion activities at the beginning, middle, or end of a unit. It can also be a strong introduction to a writing exercise or a review for a test.

A seminar on a short text dealing with our place in the environment (see right) or issues of environmentalism would work as a nice introduction to this section.

Theme—Our Relationship to
the Environment

Unit—Weather

- Continue project work: students plan and execute their own Weather Show for videotaping
- Finish reading *Thunder Cake*

- Teacher-led discussion of story (*Thunder Cake*)
- What's the role of the environment in *our* lives?
- Back in groups: continue project work

A seminar in place of this discussion can accomplish the same curricular objectives…

…but with all the child-centered cognitive and affective enhancements of a seminar.

Other possible seminar texts for this unit:
- Many teachers have had great success with maps and graphs. The NASA home page on the World Wide Web can take you to some *incredible* weather photos (check under "weather," "hurricanes," and "satellite photos").
- Selections from *House at Pooh Corner*
- "Icarus and Daedelus"
- For advanced classes: *Hatchet* or *The Cay*

FIGURE 4.3. INTEGRATING SEMINARS:
ELEVENTH GRADE SOCIAL STUDIES

Begin ch. 5 on the Constitution	◆ *Pop quiz* on homework	◆ Lecture: "The People Involved"
◆ Discuss conditions that led to the writing of the document	◆ Get into groups and begin Model Constitutional Convention project	◆ Continue group work
◆ *Homework*:	◆ In groups: assign leaders, pick areas of interest	◆ Designate group recorders
• Read Preamble and Article I		◆ Groups will decide on their part of the project
• Answer questions 1–10 on page 54	◆ Distribute contracts	◆ Groups contract for their grades
	◆ *Homework:* read Article II	

A seminar could be used *in place of* this activity as a pre-reading "anticipatory set" exercise.

If the introductory reading is assigned ahead of time, such a seminar can essentially cover the same ideas (remember: *you* are still asking the questions), but will do so in a student-centered, more democratic manner.

- Continue group work:
  - Groups should finish the design of their involvement
  - Each member's role must be spelled out in contract
- *Homework*: read pages 55–62; do questions 6–8

- *Pop quiz* on reading
- Lecture: "economic climate"
- Back into groups to continue project

Or, if Monday's discussion really *needs* to be teacher-centered (as is sometimes the case), you might decide to have a seminar here.

In this case, a seminar on a significant passage of the homework reading could serve to deepen understanding *as well as* enhance the quality of the project.

Possible seminar texts for this unit:
- A section of the Constitution*
- One of Jefferson's letters from the period
- Contemporary map of the states
- Ben Franklin's "Address to the Federal Convention" of 1787*
- "Hamilton's Plan for Union" (presented to the Convention on June 18, 1787)*

*Available in Daniel Boorstin's *An American Primer*

THE STUDENT

The ultimate goal of the seminar is to facilitate the students' learning to read critically, listen closely, respond thoughtfully, clarify their statements, and justify their thinking—all for themselves. All of these skills need to be coached continuously in the Paideia classroom, both as a part of formal seminar behavior and as solid learning behavior in non-seminar settings.

The student's first job is to read the text carefully at least twice and to mark it liberally with notes and questions. Dynamic reading of a worthy text all but guarantees a successful seminar.

During the seminar itself, the student's role is that of a respectful and reflective participant in the discussion. Most experienced leaders establish a set of general guidelines (often adapted to fit the individual situation) that foster conversation, but rich participation is more a matter of experience and dedication to mutual learning than it is strict adherence to a set of rules.

The student's first job during the seminar itself is to answer the questions posed by the seminar leader. In considering how best to coach students in this skill, seminar leaders may want to keep in mind that their goal is to elicit *thoughtful* responses. Experienced seminar participants learn to think before they speak, anticipating the objections and questions of others. Seen in this light, the value of the students' careful reading of the text becomes more obvious.

Careful preparation and thoughtful participation lead to the third student task: asking honest, thought-provoking questions as a natural part of the discussion. The difference here, of course, is that students are, in fact, questioning each other, not the teacher. A good seminar is a not a debate in which one individual or team vanquishes another with superior logic or vehemence. Rather, it is a cooperative venture in which everyone's understanding of the text should be enhanced whether they come to agree or disagree. To maximize learning during the seminar, a participant has to be willing to be wrong—realize an error, accept superior logic, and respond to someone else's insight. A good seminar has a synergy in which one participant's insight fuels another's, culminating in a kind of domino effect and taking all the participants deeper into the ideas and values of the text than any of them could have gone alone.

Finally, good seminar participants realize that a seminar rarely ends in definite answers and official positions. If a leader has chosen an evocative, multifaceted text full of profound issues—a classic—then the participants will naturally reject an artificial schoolroom closure to their search. With only a little encouragement and training, students will adopt the attitude that a good seminar initiates a rich relationship with a text, not closes it.

THE CROW AND THE PITCHER: AN ELEMENTARY SCIENCE SEMINAR

Imagine a cold October morning in a suburban elementary school in Mentor, Ohio. The first-grade teacher is reading Aesop's fable "The Crow and the Pitcher" to 28 students. This reading is the second of the morning, and the students are listening closely because they know they are about to participate in a "seminar," or, as one student calls it, a "sin-a-mar." After the reading, which tells the story of a thirsty crow who is frustrated because he cannot get any of the cool, refreshing water he discovers in a pitcher, the teacher asks half the class to draw and color the crow solving the problem of the pitcher. In the fable, the crow hits upon the solution of dropping pebbles into the pitcher until the level of the water rises sufficiently so that the crow can drink.

The other half of the class sits in a circle on the rug in the reading corner. There the teacher asks students this opening question: What other sorts of animals besides the crow might be able to solve the problem of the pitcher, and how might they solve it? The children come up with wildly creative ideas, many of which relate directly to the physical characteristics of the animal under discussion and/or the pitcher with its narrow mouth. After they have talked for awhile, the teacher, being careful to elicit at least one idea from each child, gets out her "props" for today's seminar: a clear gallon milk jug and a bag of rocks. She fills the jug partway with water and asks a child to mark the water level on the side with a magic marker. She strews the gravel from the bag on the carpet and then lets the children in the circle put all the rocks in the milk jug.

Once all the rocks are collected and placed in the jug, she again has a child mark the water level. Once the children have realized just how much the water level has actually risen (they are usually quite surprised), she asks them the primary conceptual question of the seminar: What happened when the crow dropped the pebbles in the pitcher of water? It takes the children about 10 minutes more of head-scratching as they struggle to articulate how the rocks "displace" the water so that it rises. They listen closely to each other because the teacher reminds them several times that they are trying to create an answer *together*. Once they have explained it to each other clearly enough, the teacher asks them to switch places with the artists and draw the crow and its pitcher but with this addition—in their drawings, they should show what happens when the pebbles are dropped into the water.

The teacher then repeats the process with the second group of children who had been drawing. In some ways, the comments of the second group are different because they have already "visualized" the problem and, perhaps, the solution. Of course, they have also heard many of their classmates' comments. After both groups have had a 15-minute seminar on the text, complete with the hands-on activity, the entire class shares their drawings, again seeking to explain with the help of their pictures the concept of displacement.

This scenario, repeated many times in elementary classrooms across the country, suggests several things about primary grades seminars: they are often fairly short, involving half of the class, rather than the whole class; they often involve art as well as writing in the postseminar activities; and they often involve at least one hands-on activity. It is important to remember, however, that just because five- and six-year-old children sometimes lack the vocabulary to express all they can see and understand does not mean that they don't live full, very active intellectual lives.

THE PERIODIC TABLE OF THE ELEMENTS:
A CHEMISTRY ONE SEMINAR

A chemistry teacher at a rural high school in North Carolina uses a seminar on the Periodic Table of the Elements as part of a comprehensive review at the end of the first grading period. She has students review their notes on the Periodic Table and prepare a written answer to the opening seminar question as homework the night before the seminar. The opening question is: Which component of the Table (horizontal or vertical rows, color coding of the elements in groups, numbering by atomic number, etc.) provides the most important information about the elements.

At the beginning of the seminar she randomly seats the students around the circle and asks them to share their prepared responses in pairs. One spokesperson from each pair summarizes the group's answers and the seminar begins. The teacher facilitates a discussion designed to elicit as much information about the Table as possible, encouraging students to take notes on a photocopy she provides each student. Core questions emphasize how the various kinds of information encoded in the Table are related—both in atomic theory and in the Table itself.

The closing question for students (again first discussed in pairs) is: How could the Table be redesigned to better represent all that we now know about the elements? The post-seminar exercise involves writing exam questions that will elicit the most sophisticated responses about the Table as possible. The teacher reports that these are almost always essay questions and that she almost always uses one of them as the essay question for her exam.

In addition to illustrating the use of a graphic text in a high school science class, this example highlights how many teachers are using seminars on seminal texts to review for summary tests or performances. The seminar works well in this role because it requires that students first analyze and then synthesize the key concepts that undergird a body of knowledge.

THE CLASSROOM

Seminar participants should sit as nearly as possible in a circle or hollow square so that the leader and all the participants can see everyone else clearly. Figure 4.4 illustrates several seating arrangements. As a general rule, the leader is best seated in the circle with the participants, so that the leader does not assume, symbolically, the role of authority figure. The rationale for the seminar circle is to make it easier for all of the students to address their classmates (not the teacher). It is for this reason that the circle is a better arrangement than the oval, the square, the rectangle, or other designs. Because this seating arrangement so enhances free and open discussion, if a teacher's classroom doesn't permit it, then the teacher should seek another location in the school to hold seminar discussions.

Ultimately, the seminar can serve as the capstone experience in powerful coached projects. It is within the context of the seminar circle that students come to understand the profound implications of what they are learning and so make it their own.

FIGURE 4.4. SEMINAR SEATING

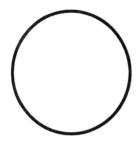

A circular arrangement of chairs or desks works best for a seminar because it allows free and equal eye contact among all the participants and allows the leader equal visual access to each participant.

When classroom shape or furniture design makes a circle impossible, a hollow square is preferable to a rectangle because it maintains equidistance among participants and allows most participants to make eye contact.

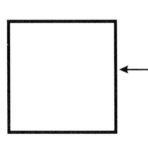

The optimal place for the seminar leader to sit in a square is midway down one side where eye contact is easily maintained with all but a few participants immediately to the leader's right or left.

In some instances, classroom shape dictates a rectangular seminar configuration. In this case, the best place for a leader to sit is halfway down one side so that the leader maintains eye contact with the most participants.

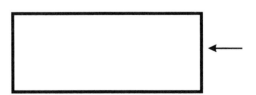

5

ASSESSMENT

When the Paideia Group composed the original Paideia Principles in the mid-1980s, it tied assessment directly to the three "columns" of instruction and the student knowledge, skill, and understanding that was supposed to result. The Group's ninth principle states:

> Each student's achievement of these results would be evaluated in terms of that student's competencies and not solely related to the achievement of other students.

This principle clearly suggests that although Paideia teachers set high standards, they do not equate intellectual quality with standardized test scores. Rather, they measure each child's progress individually and communicate about that progress as clearly and helpfully as possible. A Paideia classroom honors the democratic ideal: it is sensitive to the rights and needs of the individual while building a sense of community for the entire group. Ultimately, how teachers assess a student's progress may well be the key to how that student responds to didactic instruction, project work, and seminar participation.

Traditional forms of evaluation stress the teacher's obligation to measure a student's knowledge and skill at key points during the year—at the end of chapters or thematic units, and at midterm and final exams. The teacher is the authority in the classroom and holds power over how and when students are "graded." This pattern often renders students passive, even resentful of classroom practice. A Paideia teacher does judge the relative quality of student work, but his or her classroom also features teacher self- and peer-assessment, student self- and peer-assessment, and, perhaps most powerful of all, collaborative assessment by all involved of their common work. This far more comprehensive, more educational process is ongoing from the first day of school to the last. Furthermore, it features a wide range of assessment practices and tools, many of which are used outside the classroom. It is built on two assumptions: that the teacher is a model learner and that students must learn to take responsibility for the quality of their own work. Ultimately, redefining the role of the teacher and the student means redefining how they communicate with each other at every level —and that communication is, in the final analysis, the core of evaluation and assessment.

To clarify how a Paideia teacher redesigns quality control in the classroom, it is instructive to differentiate between the terms *assessment* and *evaluation*—both vital elements of Paideia teaching. Giving feedback and judging quality are as natural to the teaching cycle as listening is to speaking. In a Paideia classroom, assessment and evaluation involve both the individual and the group, based on the display of knowledge, skill, and understanding. Assessment and evaluation, therefore, align with didactic instruction, coaching, and seminar by utilizing a variety of tools that provide feedback.

Assessment in the Paideia classroom refers to a cyclical process (see Figure 5.1) that involves teachers and students working together to:

♦ Identify their curriculum goals

♦ Diagnose their status relative to those goals

♦ Plan strategies to achieve those goals

♦ Measure progress along the way

Assessment feedback is ongoing and exists in most instructional conversations as well as in written responses to teacher and student work. Assessment indicates to the individual and group where they are in relation to their goals. In the Paideia classroom, assessment provides teachers, students, and parents with a clear sense of *individual* student progress.

Evaluation adds an additional step to the assessment process. Evaluation includes value judgments about individual and group status and usually occurs at the end of a unit, a

**Figure 5.1. The Cycle of Assessment
and Evaluation**

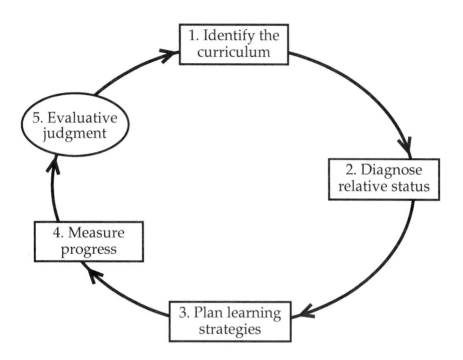

grading period, or a semester. Evaluation in a Paideia classroom often provides the specific grades that students and parents expect on report cards and progress reports. Often, it clarifies a student's progress relative to other students of the same age or grade.

It is important for teachers to understand that assessment and evaluation are not mutually exclusive events; rather they complement each other, with evaluative information often serving as the benchmark for a new learning cycle, and the assessment process anticipating and informing evaluation. Many measurement tools—quizzes, tests, discussions, essays, products—are part of the assessment process and also help determine a student's grade. When a Paideia teacher gives a brief quiz in the middle of a coached project, the teacher may use the information gleaned to decide whether a key body of information or skill (assessment) needs to be retaught, and the teacher may later factor the student scores into the final project grade (evaluation). Again the Paideia classroom features a range of assessment activities: teacher self- and peer-assessment, student self- and peer-assessment, and collaborative assessment of common work (see Figure 5.2).

Earlier chapters were organized around the roles of teachers versus those of students, but assessment in the Paideia classroom is based on students and teachers working together to guarantee ongoing improvement toward common goals. This chapter examines assessment in each column of instruction in turn.

Just as it helps teachers to think about didactic instruction, coaching, and seminar leadership as three separate skills to be mastered, it helps to understand Paideia assessment in those same three categories.

DIDACTIC INSTRUCTION

Paideia teachers often use homework assignments to enhance and measure student response to didactic lessons; they often use traditional tools like quizzes and tests to measure both student comprehension and retention of basic information. They use these instruments not only to measure student progress at the end of units of study but also to gauge

FIGURE 5.2. THE ASSESSMENT KALEIDOSCOPE

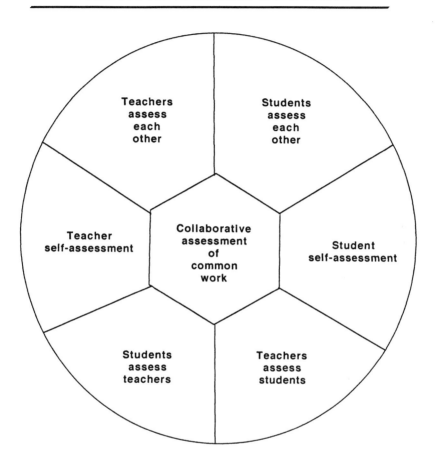

comprehension early in a unit in order to decide how well prepared their students are to go on to the more complex activities and applications involved in projects and seminars. Most evaluation of didactic teaching and learning involves the more traditional construct of teachers testing students: retention and comprehension via quizzes and multiple-choice, short answer tests, and so forth.

THE COACHED PROJECT

The more comprehensive and sophisticated coached project involves a wide variety of assessment constructs: teacher assessing students, students assessing teacher, as well as student peer- and self-assessment. It also involves a wide range of assessment tools: time lines, calendar deadlines, checklists, rubrics, and portfolios. Because the product orientation of the coached project requires whole-class planning, design, and effort, it also stresses the sort of collaborative, ongoing assessment that in many ways captures the very heart of the assessment concept. Because the nature of the coached project is to work toward a common product of the highest quality, students and teacher together must stop consistently along the way to measure their progress relative to a quality prototype (see Chapter 2). Thus, the tools that they can use together— time lines, deadlines, checklists, rubrics—become vital to the process (see Appendix C). Often, they must together design these tools to fit specific projects/products so that the students grow in their ability to create, as well as to apply, quality control measures. The students can even help design the quizzes and tests that measure their increasing mastery of the information and skills involved.

SEMINAR

In several regards, the seminar completes both the spectrum of instruction and the cycle of assessment. It adds an uncommon depth to student understanding to a unit of study. And because a seminar is most powerful within a coached project, students and teachers assess the seminar process and content both before and after the seminar discussion itself, thereby integrating the seminar into the project. Good pre-

and post-seminar assessments of the individual and group participation in the process are full of self- and peer-assessment, both by teachers as well as students. In addition to the other tools commonly associated with didactic and coached learning, seminars often feature oral examination and writing as common modes of evaluation—activities that measure the depth of a student's understanding of sophisticated concepts. In part because a seminar produces a highly personal understanding rather than consensus, it is all but impossible to measure the resulting growth with any instrument that doesn't allow students to express complex and highly individualized thought.

To coach the process of seminar participation, however, Paideia teachers use checklists of leader and participant behaviors, as well as rubrics, to gauge growing mastery of those skills (see Appendix C). Increasingly, they are using the resulting information to construct teacher and student seminar portfolios. In addition to the self and collaborative assessments that characterize coached projects, these assessments teach students to increasingly accept responsibility for the quality of their individual work and that of the common discussion.

JAMES MCINTYRE:
HIGH SCHOOL SEMINAR STUDENT

James McIntyre is a fictional student in Alicia Fernandino's geometry class in a Ft. Lauderdale, Florida, urban high school. His teacher is committed to using seminar instruction to introduce the math concepts that each chapter brings to her students. She is in her third year of using seminars for math instruction and, working with students, she has developed a checklist (see Figure 5.3) of learning behaviors for her math seminars that is stapled to the inside back cover of each student's seminar folder. The items on the checklist are:

- ◆ Conduct
  - • Listens respectfully
  - • Invites comment
  - • Does not interrupt

FIGURE 5.3. CHECKLIST GRID OF PAIDEIA SEMINAR BEHAVIORS

Name __James McIntyre__

Class __3rd Period Geometry__

Text	Euclid, Bk 1	Euclid, Bk 2	Landscape Painting	3 square Root	Prob. 32 Page 112	Coke Can Prob	Pyramid Prob								
Date	9/3	9/11	9/23	10/8	10/21	11/16	11/29								
Conduct															
Listens Respect.	✓	✓	✓		✓	✓	✓								
Invites Comment					✓	✓	✓								
Does not Interrupt				✓		✓	✓ ✓-								

Speaking/Reasoning

- Speaks >3 times
- Refers to Text
- Asks Questions
- Explains, Justifies

Listening

- Looks at Speaker
- Follows Textual
- References
- Asks Follow-up Questions

Reading

- Takes Notes on Text
- Prepares Open Statement — But often Doesn't share

- ◆ Speaking/Reasoning
  - Speaks at least three times
  - Refers to text
  - Asks questions
  - Explains and justifies
- ◆ Listening
  - Looks at speaker
  - Follows textual references
  - Asks follow-up questions
- ◆ Reading
  - Takes notes on text
  - Prepares opening statement

Early in the fall semester, James was reluctant to speak in seminar even though he has always been a good math student. He is a shy young man who often stutters when asked to read or speak in front of an entire class. For this reason, he often writes notes during seminar, jotting down a response and passing it to a student next to him, encouraging his neighbor to read his response aloud, even to take credit for it so no attention will come his way.

Ms. Fernandino realized within the first few weeks of the semester why James was so reluctant to talk in class and began to encourage him to prepare answers in advance to seminar questions she wrote out for him. She asked him to practice reading his answers so that he could relay them comfortably to rest of the class during the discussion. She also seated him between two of his friends in the seminar circle, two students who did not understand geometry as well as James, so that when she asked "paired" seminar questions,[1] James would feel more comfortable speaking and could share his insights with others.

During September and October, James consistently scored a positive response to checklist items related to prepara-

---

1. A "paired" seminar question refers to a question that the seminar leader asks pairs of students to first discuss together before sharing their answers with the entire group.

tion and listening, but he was never able to record that he had spoken during the seminar. As he became increasingly aware of his responsibility to share his insight, however, he began to speak during the early stages of Ms. Fernandino's seminars, at first only once or twice per discussion and only barely above a whisper. But with her encouragement and, just as importantly, that of his friends, he began to speak more and more often, even interrupting a classmate during an early December seminar, an event that elicited a round of applause from his classmates.

Ms. Fernandino's consistent use of a checklist grid for all her students had become, for James, the one constant reminder that he needed to improve his ability to share ideas orally, not only for his sake but for that of every other participant in the seminar circle. And at the end of the semester, he asked her if he could take his seminar checklist(Figure 5.3) home with his report card. He was, he said, more proud of learning to talk in seminar than he was of his grade in the class.

Just as a full, three-column unit of study integrates all three modes of Paideia instruction so that they complement each other, that same unit integrates all the forms of teacher and student assessment into an ongoing and collaborative review of common work. This collaboration is so important because it decreases the distance between teacher and student so that the teacher becomes a much more powerful role model—modeling the habit of lifelong learning that should become the hallmark of a Paideia classroom.

6

SPEAKING AND LISTENING IN THE CLASSROOM

One way to clearly picture how Paideia teachers progress with their students is to imagine the classroom conversations that produce more compelling projects and more profound seminars. This chapter contains three dramatized dialogues. The first shows a third grade teacher in a rural North Carolina school "intellectually coaching" (see Chapter 3 and Appendix B) his students as they work together with community members on a coached project. The second dialogue captures the post-seminar reflections (see Chapter 4 and Appendix C) of a group of eleventh grade American history students and their teacher following a seminar on the "Emancipation Proclamation." The third dialogue shows how ideas are generated in a seminar discussion. Although these dialogues are imaginary, they are based on a number of actual projects and seminars and so reflect the reality of interaction.

WHAT LAST NIGHT'S STORM TAUGHT US: INTELLECTUAL COACHING IN THE THIRD GRADE

Jim Morgan's third grade class had taken on a real-world problem as the basis for their science unit on weather and erosion. The six-foot high, red clay bank that separated the playground from the back of their school had begun eroding the year before and was creeping closer to the building with every rain storm. Mr. Morgan's challenge to his students was to develop a method to stabilize the bank and, working with parent volunteers, prevent further erosion.

To develop their ideas, the students first studied erosion in a water table they built in the classroom. Mr. Morgan then divided the class into five design teams, each of which was to develop a model for the system that they thought would solve the problem. After the groups had developed their ideas by drawing and writing detailed descriptions and explanations of why they thought their designs would work, a 25-foot segment of the bank was divided into five sections. One Friday afternoon each group, working with parent volunteers, stabilized its section of the bank using the method it had developed. One group used drain pipe and gravel; one used rye grass; one used larger rock stabilized with chicken wire, one used railroad ties to build terraces, and one used a combination of several methods.

In addition to Mr. Morgan and his students, his assessment team—the school's maintenance chief and a local landscaper—also visited to see the five prototypes. Once the five designs were in place, all waited for it to rain.

On a Thursday night two weeks later, a hard rainstorm came through the area, and the rain didn't stop until mid-morning on Friday. It is now 11:00 AM, and Mr. Morgan and his students are on the playground with cameras and clipboards, comparing the results. To get the students to think objectively about their designs, Mr. Morgan divides them into four research teams (each of which has at least one member of each original design team). The research teams are to rank the five designs according to cost, ease of construction, appearance, and effectiveness. Because of their interest in the project, several parents, the local landscaper, and the principal have also stopped by to examine the results of the rain storm.

Mr. Morgan and Ms. Betts, the landscaper, are questioning one of the research teams as they compare the rye grass section to the more elaborate drain pipe and gravel construction.

Mr. Morgan: "Which worked the best?"

Jeffrey: "They both worked. We think these two worked better than any others."

Mr. Morgan: "Okay. If they worked equally well, what else do you have to consider?"

Gina: "How much they cost. And how they look...."

Mr. Morgan: "And...?"

Ms. Betts, standing behind Mr. Morgan, silently flexes her muscles and pantomimes digging with a shovel.

Gina: "Ease of construction!"

Mr. Morgan (laughing): "That's three ways you need to compare them. Now put your heads together and come up with a conclusion. If we're going to do the whole bank with one method, which method should it be?"

The children try to pull Ms. Betts into their group to help. She good-naturedly listens but, as she's been coached by Mr. Morgan, she refuses to answer their questions. A few minutes later, Mr. Morgan returns from coaching another research group.

Mr. Morgan: "Well, what did you decide?"

Chuck: "The gravel costs a lot more than the grass seed and straw and it's a lot harder to throw out gravel than it is to plant grass."

Ms. Betts: "But didn't one group have to keep coming back out to work on their section?"

Mr. Morgan: "Kept having to spend their recess...."

Chuck: "Our group! We had to keep coming back to water the grass."

Mr. Morgan: "So . . . ?"

Chuck: "But it didn't take that long and (the students whisper together for a moment)...we still think grass is easier."

Mr. Morgan: "Which do you think looks better? And remember what we talked about in class. Don't just pick one over the other but take notes on why. (He turns to Ms. Betts.) What questions are we forgetting to ask?"

Ms. Betts (speaking directly to the group): "Which of the two do you think will last? You don't want to keep doing this job over and over."

As she begins talking with the students, the principal, Dr. Johnson, walks up to the group.

Dr. Johnson: "Mr. Morgan, good news. The maintenance supervisor just called to find out about the
project. He said the county maintenance crew
would implement whichever design the children
chose."

Mr. Morgan: "That's—"

But before he can speak, the children interrupt him.

Children: "No, no! We have to do the work ourselves!
It's our project!"

Dr. Johnson (to Mr. Morgan): "But should you take that
much time away from your other school work?"

Gina (before he can speak): "We're doing all our math
and reading on erosion already."

Ms. Betts: "Besides, the kids already talked about it.
They want to do the work on a Saturday, so they
won't have to give up any more recess. But if they're
right, what the county can provide is—"

Chuck: "A ton of grass seed!"

"WHEN YOU HAVE THE IDEA YOURSELF...": POST-SEMINAR REFLECTION IN THE ELEVENTH GRADE

There are 10 minutes left in Ms. Franklin's eleventh grade
American History and Government class. Ms. Franklin and
her 32 students have just finished a seminar on the Emancipation Proclamation that is part of a unit on the American Civil
War. The unit itself is being planned and implemented in the
form of a coached project: the product is a readers' theater
production about how those who were present remember
Lincoln's Gettysburg Address.

During their preseminar preparation, students had shad-
ed a map showing those areas of the country where the Proclamation had "freed" the slaves and those areas where it had
not. In addition, students had done their typical preparation
of the text: two readings with close note-taking and the iden-
tification and study of difficult vocabulary. Preseminar dis-

cussion had focused on what the Emancipation Proclamation revealed about Lincoln's character (a content focus; note the connection to the eventual coached product) and on how the group would stress references to the text during the discussion (a process focus).

The seminar has been observed by Ms. Franklin's "peer coach," Bill Cheshire, a young second-year teacher who completed seminar training just the summer before. He has been taking notes furiously during the discussion.

Ms. Franklin: "Before we break up, I want to debrief."

(Groans from the students, many of whom are still lost in thought from the seminar's closing moments.)

Ms. Franklin: "Take out your journals. Write for a few moments on these two process questions. One, did we succeed in referring more consistently to the text? Two, were you personally a better participant than in recent seminars? Why or why not?"

(Students start writing. As they do, Mr. Cheshire tiptoes to Ms. Franklin who is seated in the circle.)

Mr. Cheshire (whispering): "How much of this had you lectured on?"

Ms. Franklin (also whispering): "Not much. They drew the map that identified the territories and did the background research on Seward."

Mr. Cheshire: "Yeah, but all those comments about personal freedom. And about education...."

Ms. Franklin: "Well, we always talk about the power of an education, but—"

Mr. Cheshire (nodding): "I thought so."

(As he turns to go back to his chair:)

Ms. Franklin (to the students): "How are we doing? Anybody ready to share?"

(Several students have been quietly coaching a shy girl in the seminar circle and now point to her.)

Several students: "Maria wants to summarize."

Ms. Franklin: "Maria? Did you volunteer or were you drafted?"

Maria: "I can do it. *We* think that, as a whole, we did a much better job of referring to the text....Your making us conscious of it helped and we reminded each other of it a time or two....But I noticed something else today. It's easy to refer to the text when the text is this interesting. Some of the seminar texts this year...."

Michael: "Just don't give us much to refer to."

Ms. Franklin: "So, what you're telling me is that a better text is fuller, deeper,...."

Maria: "Has a lot more stuff to work through so we almost have to refer to it more."

Ms. Franklin: "Thank you....Who has some individual insight to share?"

Davida: "I was *not* as good a seminar participant today as in previous seminars because...."

Another student: "Because?"

Davida: "I talked so much. I couldn't get over what a political operator Lincoln was, and I ran my mouth way too much."

(General laughter.)

Ms. Franklin: "We'll forgive you this once. Anybody *succeed* in improving?"

Marcus: "I listened much better this time. Partly because of the text, partly because I made myself take notes. Taking notes on what everybody else says really helps me."

Ms. Franklin: "Thank you, Marcus. We're running out of time. For homework, I want you all to take some notes in your seminar log books on what you learned today about Lincoln. His personality? His politics? His surroundings? Also, I want to thank...."

(She sees Cheshire, who's frantically trying to get her attention.) Mr. Cheshire?"

Mr. Cheshire: "I want to ask a question. How much of what you all said about education—the power of an education to set an individual free—came from what Ms. Franklin has told you before?"

Davida (speaking for several students who seem almost insulted): "You mean you can't believe we could think those things for ourselves?"

Mr. Cheshire: "No...well, yes. I was impressed, but...."

Marcus: "Mr. Cheshire, we talk about the power of an education and personal choice in here all the time. As a theme in American history, but...."

Ms. Franklin: "What Marcus is trying to say, Mr. Cheshire, is that although we've discussed how education and spirituality free an individual, nobody —including me—had ever applied it to slavery or to the Proclamation until Maria said what she did in today's seminar."

Maria (obviously emotional): "I said that Lincoln couldn't free the slaves. He could only give them the right to pursue their own freedom as individuals."

Davida: "Through learning to read and write. Through learning to control their own lives. Through—"

Marcus (who is still taking notes): "Mr. Cheshire, no matter how many times in history someone has had an idea, when you have an idea the first time yourself, it's so new it hurts."

Davida (echoing a class theme): "Hurts like growing pains! These *are* our ideas because what seminars do is let you give birth to the ideas yourself."

The bell rings. Ms. Franklin thanks her students as they rise to go.

SEMINAR DISCUSSION: HOW IDEAS ARE GENERATED

C.J. Anderson's ninth grade Government class is in the middle of a seminar on the Preamble to the Constitution. This is the third seminar of the year for this particular class and the first that has really gone well, with nearly all the students participating voluntarily, building idea on top of idea. Anderson began the seminar by asking each student to name the single concept in the Preamble that was most important in a democracy:

> We the people of the United States, in order to form a more perfect union, establish justice, insure domestic tranquility, provide for the common defense, promote the general welfare, and secure the blessings of liberty to ourselves and our posterity, do ordain and establish this Constitution for the United States of America.

During the original round-robin response, a student volunteer listed the concepts on the board, tallying multiple votes for particular concepts. Thirty-two students responded as follows:

We/people	9
Justice	5
Union	1
Tranquility	1
Common defense	4
Liberty	7
United	2
Welfare (general)	1

Anderson then opened the seminar for general discussion, asking students to explain why they chose certain concepts as important to democracy. The conversation was lively, and he was pleased to see his students thinking clearly about democracy as a form of government.

Thirty minutes into the seminar, Jeremy, normally a very quiet student, pointed out that all the concepts are related:

Jeremy: It's like no one of these equals a democracy. It's as if you had, say, "domestic tranquility"; tranquility could exist under a dictator. That one element alone doesn't make a democracy.

Maria: I think I see what Jeremy means. We could "provide for the common defense" with a military government. Maybe even better than with a democracy....So it takes all of these working together to produce democracy.

Mr. Anderson: Okay, but how? Look at the concepts that Janine listed on the board earlier. Eight ideas: My question is *how* are they related to each other?

Monte: For one thing, liberty and justice are related.

Mr. Anderson: How?

Monte: A strong justice system protects us from each other. It's what keeps us from beating each other up in the halls, stealing from each other. It's what keeps me from taking someone else's liberty away.

Juanita: Or someone else from taking yours.

Monte: Exactly

George: It's as if in a democracy we're all connected somehow. What's good for you is also good for me.

Janine: Is that why nine of us voted for "we the people" as the most important concept in the whole thing?

William: Has to be. I voted for it originally, but I was never able to explain why. It's strange, but none of those concepts work if we're at war with each other. It's only when we work collaboratively that any of these ideas have a chance.

The students laugh. *Collaborative* is a buzz word that Anderson has drilled into them.

Juanita: But look at the board: *union, common* defense. It's like the theme of the whole Preamble is that somehow we are all tied together.

Mr. Anderson: Look back at the Preamble to see if Juanita is right. Is unit a common theme?

Jean: "A more perfect union...."

Anthony: "Common...general...."

Helen: Oh, oh, I see it. "The *United* States of America."

Tony: Tranquility is connected, too. I think people are more willing to get along during times of peace and tranquility.

Micha: Then common defense is important to unity. It's a strong defense that keeps us safe enough. Stable enough to care for and help each other.

Megan: Justice also unites people. I know that when I think I've been treated unjustly, it infuriates me, and usually I'm infuriated at someone. Mad at the world.

Jean: I want to say I think it's neat that all of this is in one sentence. I don't think it's an accident that all of these ideas are "united" in one sentence.

The seminar goes on for another 20 minutes before winding down. In the post-seminar phase, students agreed to work together to write a preamble to a class constitution, a project that Anderson had suggested earlier in the year.

During the post-seminar discussion of the seminar process, Jose admitted that early in the seminar he had talked more than he usually did, and Anderson asked why he'd fallen silent for the last half.

Jose: It's like my mind was flooded with ideas. Once we started talking about how all those concepts were related, every time I opened my mouth to speak, ten thoughts raced across my mind at once, and I didn't know where to begin....But I'll tell you one thing; I've got so many notes, I think I could write a class preamble all by myself.

7

INSTRUCTIONALLY INTEGRATED UNITS

When the National Paideia Center trains teachers in the three-columns of teaching and learning, the first focus is usually on the seminar as a formal teaching ritual to be used on a regular basis with students so that it becomes a positive and eagerly anticipated part of the classroom culture. Initial research suggests that middle and high school students derive the greatest benefit from a consistent, schoolwide implementation of the seminar, but individual teachers can certainly use the seminar as a teaching technique with positive results in only their classrooms. To give beginning seminar leaders the best possible chance for success, introductory training should include observation, participation, and practice leadership that is followed by regular observation and coaching from an experienced leader during the year.

Once teachers are comfortable using seminars in the classroom, they are introduced to the more comprehensive concept of project-oriented coaching and, typically in the second year of a Paideia implementation plan, write product-directed projects into their academic curriculums. With these two student-centered teaching techniques at their disposal, teachers can then dramatically reduce the amount of didactic teaching they do and emphasize quality instead of quantity.

Teachers can then build coherent three-column unit plans that focus both on what will be taught and on how that curriculum will be delivered. It is at this point that teachers can begin to use each of the three columns to its best effect by applying it when and where it is most appropriate: didactic instruction to introduce a body of information; coached projects to practice the intellectual skills involved in applying the information; and the seminar to focus on manipulating ideas and values inherent to the information.

Because of the pressures created by standardized curriculums and testing programs, many educators feel the need to align their curriculum with that of the state or district. What may ultimately determine how successfully they teach that curriculum, however, is instructional alignment and integration. Eventually we ask all Paideia teachers to first consider how best to teach any lesson—whether through didactic, coached, or seminar instruction—and then to integrate all three forms of instruction into a seamless unit of study.

What teachers and administrators discover along the way is that the implementation of the three columns may call into question traditional notions of scheduling, assessment, and student tracking. An intense didactic lesson requires less time than the traditional 55-minute junior or senior high school block, but both coached projects and the seminar require longer blocks of time. Because of this need for more time, the use of block scheduling in American middle and high schools has freed many teachers to experiment more fully with these two columns.

New ways of thinking about the roles of teacher and student also make traditional forms of assessment and reporting seem incomplete if not downright obsolete. Certainly, redefining student work in both the coached project (whether alone or as part of a group) and seminar requires new and better ways to measure and nurture that work and for better ways of reporting the progress of that work to students and their parents. For this reason, Paideia schools typically move quickly toward more authentic forms of assessment either in place of or in addition to traditional evaluation.

Finally, Adler is adamant about schools offering the same quality, not merely the same quantity, of education for all students. He is publicly opposed to most forms of tracking and ability grouping as both elitist and counterproductive. This element of *The Paideia Proposal* is borne out in the application of the three columns of teaching and learning because both the coached project and the seminar work best when implemented with heterogeneous groups of students. Here, again, most Paideia schools come to examine their student placement policies within the first few years of implementation and many move toward a program of full or partial inclusion and full or partial heterogeneous grouping for all subjects.

Because so many of the changes that naturally result from implementing the three columns of teaching and learning involve systemic, schoolwide reform, Paideia teachers and Paideia classrooms tend to survive, and eventually thrive, in a schoolwide Paideia program. Additionally, research has shown that students derive the most benefit from the teaching practices when they encounter them consistently from class to class and from year to year. Ultimately, then, the three columns are not just teaching techniques; they are integral parts of a larger reform plan that has implications for every aspect of school life and implications for enriching the learning of us all—adult and child alike.

EVIDENCE

Research on the effectiveness of Paideia school reform dates from mid-1982 to contemporary efforts. The studies suggest that Paideia reform impacts the climate of the classroom and school, increasing both student and teacher interest in academic study. Most of the research focuses on the seminar component of the program, because it was originally the most clearly defined of the three columns of instruction.

In 1995, Herman and Stringfield published an important report entitled *Ten Promising Programs for Educating Disadvantaged Students* through the Center for the Social Organization of Schools at Johns Hopkins. This report noted the need for schoolwide implementation of the Paideia program so that students experienced seminars and coached projects consistently. Further, it suggests the potential of the program to increase student ability to:

◆ solve problems

◆ work collaboratively with others

◆ think conceptually and coherently about a range of subjects

◆ present ideas both orally and in writing

The relationship between the Paideia seminar and thinking and writing skills is further explored by Chesser, Gellatly, and Hale in their 1997 article on Githens Middle School in Durham, North Carolina (*Middle School Journal*). These authors suggest the possibility of a strong correlation between articulation in the seminar and written articulation.

In addition, because the Paideia seminar is an actively student-centered teaching and learning technique, the studies also suggest that regular seminar instruction may cause:

♦ an increase in student interest and engagement in class work

♦ an increase in overall student interest in school

♦ lower absentee and dropout rates

Because many schools are moving toward more authentic, qualitative measures of student achievement, including asking students to write sophisticated responses instead of answering multiple-choice questions, future studies may well show consistent and measurable increases in standardized student achievement.

It is important to remember, however, that the Paideia classroom is designed to nurture the whole child—preparing the child to hold a job, become an active citizen, and lead a life rich in learning. At best, it is an environment of civility and collaboration, an incubator of lifelong, as well as short-term, learning.

APPENDICES

INTRODUCTION

Because this is a book by and for teachers, we have included the following appendices to help bring profound seminars and exciting coached projects to life in your classroom. These appendices are full of tools such as diagrams, lesson plans, seating charts, checklists, and rubrics, developed by and for teachers for use in learning how to lead quality seminars and how to facilitate coached projects. We have also included an introduction to each item that explains how and why teachers developed this particular tool and how it might be used most powerfully in your classroom.

The staff of the National Paideia Center, along with the thousands of teachers with whom we work, are constantly developing new strategies for use in the classroom and as a Paideia teacher you are now a part of that effort. We encourage you to use these appendices to enrich your learning process and then to create—with your students whenever possible—your own lesson plans, diagrams, and rubrics that can, in turn, be shared with the growing number of Paideia teachers around the country.

APPENDIX A

SEMINAR INSTRUCTION

As we worked with teachers over the past few years to develop their skills (as well as our own) as seminar leaders, it became increasingly obvious that there are at least two vitally important elements to the seminar: the content and the process. The "content" of a seminar is both the text under discussion and the ideas and values that emerge from that text. The "process" involves both the communal values of collaborative discussion and the learning skills that students must master to become able participants. Obviously, the two elements of the seminar are closely interrelated, but it is often instructive to consider both in either anticipating or reflecting on a seminar. As you work your way through the items in this Appendix, keep in mind both these important elements.

THE PAIDEIA SEMINAR

The Paideia Seminar is a formal discussion based on a text, in which the leader of the discussion asks open-ended questions designed to precipitate spirited and thoughtful dialogue. As a result, the participants are asked to articulate, justify, and clarify their own ideas as well as their responses to the ideas of others. The ultimate goal of a seminar is that all participants develop a more sophisticated understanding of the text through thoughtful interaction with the ideas of others. Neither consensus or closure should signal the end of a seminar; rather continued inquiry and reflection should flow directly out of the experience.

To participate in a seminar, a student must practice all of the traditional liberal arts—reading, writing, speaking, listening, and thinking—the skills with which we learn in any discipline. In this context, preseminar preparation by teacher and students and post-seminar assessment and writing are vital parts of a seamless process informed throughout by reflection. The seminar is flexible enough as a formal learning event that it can be used to successfully coach all of these skills, including deeper and more sophisticated levels of thought.

THE SEMINAR CIRCLE

Teachers have known since the early 1980s that the optimal seminar seating arrangement is a circle or hollow square because this allows and encourages students to focus on and talk to one another. In primary classrooms, teachers are translating this strategy into 12 or 14 students seated on a rug in the reading corner talking about a story while their classmates are working at their desks illustrating the story's themes. In crowded high school classrooms, teachers often have to leave overcrowded rooms or heavy science tables behind, running their seminars in the media center or in a quiet lobby. Over and over, teachers are finding creative ways to place their students in circles or squares that lead to open and free exchange.

During the late 1980s and early 1990s, teachers experimented with an inner circle (of students who discussed) and outer circle (who observed the discussion) as a method for dealing with class sizes in excess of 35. Experience has taught us, however, that to gain maximum benefit from the seminar students need to be directly involved in the discussion. This realization has forced teachers to seek out larger, more flexible spaces and longer seminar periods to accommodate seminars of up to 40 participants.

SEMINAR SEATING

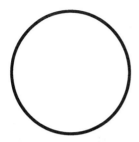

A circular arrangement of chairs or desks works best for a seminar because it allows free and equal eye contact among all the participants and allows the leader equal visual access to each participant.

When classroom shape or furniture design makes a circle impossible, a hollow square is preferable to a rectangle because it maintains equidistance among participants and allows most participants to make eye contact.

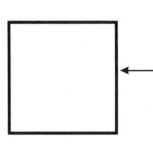

The optimal place for the seminar leader to sit in a square is midway down one side where eye contact is easily maintained with all but a few participants immediately to the leader's right or left.

In some instances, classroom shape dictates a rectangular seminar configuration. In this case, the best place for a leader to sit is halfway down one side so that the leader maintains eye contact with the most participants.

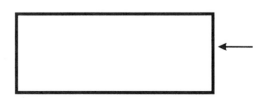

CHOOSING SEMINAR TEXTS

Because schools and teachers are held increasingly accountable by state and local authorities for measurable student achievement, Paideia teachers struggle to find seminar texts that help deliver the curricula for which they are responsible. For this reason, text discovery and selection may be one of the biggest challenges teachers face, and it is imperative that they work together to find and use texts that are both rich in conceptual content and aligned with the curriculum. Paideia teachers, more than ever before, need to network, to communicate by grade level and subject area—within and between schools—sharing those texts that teach to the conceptual potential of their common curriculum.

A strong text goes a long way toward solving the most common problems inherent to the seminar. Because a good text is evocative, it often engages a wide variety of students. Because it is thought-provoking, it often leads to a discussion of some depth.

For these and other, similar reasons, the first important step in planning any seminar is text selection. And perhaps the first question a teacher should ask when considering a text is which core ideas and values it asks us to consider. When we seek to engage students with exciting and "relevant" texts, it is important to remember that a classic, contemporary or ancient, *is* a classic primarily because it speaks to a variety of people over a significant period of time.

- A strong seminar text:
- Addresses a number of essential human concerns and so evokes a variety of responses from a variety of students;
- Is thought-provoking. It is not easy to dispose of intellectually;
- Addresses ideas and values of some complexity;
- Is evocative and often ambiguous. There is more to discussing it than simply agreeing or disagreeing with its message;

+ Deals with issues of some particular concern of the intended participants; and

+ Integrates coherently into the curriculum.

It is also important to remember that a successful seminar text is rarely simple in theme or function. It is often ambiguous enough to reward multiple readings and to all but demand shared inquiry. As you move toward more fully integrating your seminar instruction into the learning life of your classroom, identify the essential ideas in a text and then thematically align the text with the lesson or unit.

Also, don't shy away from assigning a text that is a little more difficult than your students are used to addressing and don't forget to offer students a variety of types and genres, including texts by women and minorities. One function of the seminar is to show how a teacher and students can together "read" a difficult or unfamiliar text more successfully than any individual working in isolation. Finally, regard the first few times you use a text as an authentic assessment of its worth. Some promising texts fail the acid test in the classroom; on the other hand, some only reveal their riches under the stimulus of discussion.

TEACHING CONCEPTUAL THINKING

Teachers sometimes forget to examine even their seminar texts for what Adler called the "great ideas." The list on the facing page grew out of the work that Adler and others did in preparing the original editions of the *Great Books* (Encyclopaedia Britannica, *Great Books of the Western World*, 54 volumes (Chicago: Encyclopaedia Britannica)). A valuable exercise for teachers involved in planning a seminar is to juxtapose this list with the seminar text to see how many ideas might be lurking there. Furthermore, it is instructive to use this list as a starting point and to brainstorm other important concepts (particularly from science, math, and the arts) that might be revealed by the discussion.

Ultimately, however, the most powerful use of a list like this is to plan evocative seminar questions that will elicit in-depth reflection about profoundly human issues.

102 BASIC IDEAS FOR DISCUSSION

A good seminar text should allow students to explore at least one of these ideas:

Angel	God	Memory and	Revolution
Animal	Good and	Imagination	Rhetoric
Aristocracy	Evil	Metaphysics	Same and
Art	Government	Mind	Other
Astronomy	Habit	Monarchy	Science
Beauty	Happiness	Nature	Sense
Being	History	Necessity and	Sign and
Cause	Honor	Contingency	Symbol
Chance	Hypothesis	Oligarchy	Sin
Citizen	Immortality	One and	Slavery
Constitution	Induction	Many	Soul
Courage	Infinity	Opinion	Space
Custom and	Judgment	Opposition	State
Convention	Justice	Philosophy	Temperance
Definition	Knowledge	Physics	Theology
Democracy	Labor	Pleasure and	Time
Desire	Language	Pain	Truth
Dialectic	Law	Poetry	Tyranny
Duty	Liberty	Power	Universal
Education	Life and	Principle	and
Equality	Death	Progress	Particular
Element	Logic	Prophecy	Virtue and
Emotion	Love	Prudence	Vice
Eternity	Man	Punishment	War and
Evolution	Mathematics	Quality	Peace
Experience	Matter	Quantity	Wealth
Family	Mechanics	Reasoning	Will
Fate	Medicine	Relation	Wisdom
Form		Religion	World

PRE- AND POSTSEMINAR ACTIVITIES

In addition to preparing effective questions, teachers must also learn to maximize the impact of the discussion by preparing students with effective pre- and postseminar activities that focus on both the process of democratic dialogue and the content of ideas and values. Teachers often use a planning form similar to the one on the opposite page to design a process that integrates the seminar into the learning life of the classroom

SEMINAR PLANNING FORM

Title of Seminar _____

Date _____

Level _____

Main Concepts/Issues	Preliminary Activities	Seminar	Post-Activities
		Opening:	
		Core:	
		Closing:	

Taking Notes

As seminar leadership expertise grows, it is often tempting to forego taking notes during the discussion, but the best seminar leaders consistently report that note-taking of several kinds is all but mandatory. Most practiced leaders note the students' names on a seating chart like the one on the facing page (often intentionally seating students for maximum participation), tallying the number of times each speaks during the discussion. This technique allows the teachers to focus on involving those who speak less often as the seminar progresses. Most teachers also develop their own shorthand to record significant student learning behaviors such as a "?" for questions asked, "t" for textual reference, and so on.

Furthermore, teachers also typically take notes on student comments, either on a separate sheet of paper on in the margins of the seating chart, so they can refer back to them either during the seminar (forming questions out of student statements) or in post-seminar activities. It is a significant breakthrough when students realize that the seminar reverses the standard classroom dynamic; teachers are now taking notes on what students say precisely because what they say is so important. Experienced leaders also often reserve a space to jot down further questions that flow out of the discussion.

SEMINAR SEATING CHART

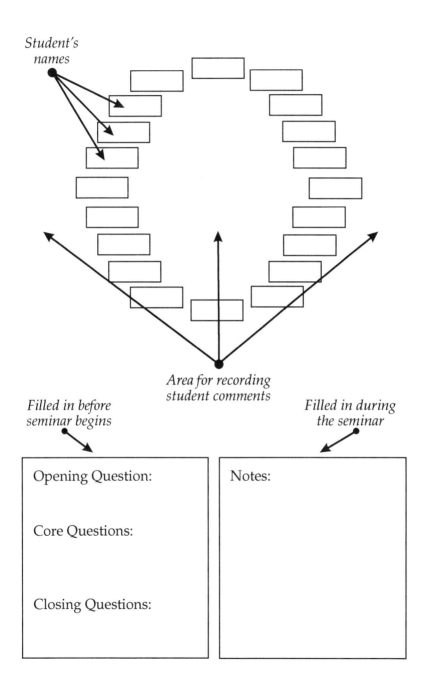

Student's names

Area for recording student comments

Filled in before seminar begins

Filled in during the seminar

Opening Question:

Core Questions:

Closing Questions:

Notes:

APPENDIX B

THE COACHED PROJECT

One of the most significant paradigm shifts that Paideia requires of a teacher is the reconfiguration of the school year into a series of coached projects. In one sense, the coached project asks teacher and students to expand the democratic climate and practices of the seminar to the rest of the school day and year. The tools we have included in this appendix are those that we have developed over the years working with teachers and students as they have planned and implemented coached projects in grades K–12.

Several of these documents reflect the nature of constructive conversations that teachers have with students as they work together through a project. Teachers "coach" students as they practice academic skills, motivated by the desire to produce quality end products.

DEFINITIONS

Teachers tell us that it helps both them and their students to clearly differentiate between "projects," "products," and the actual "coaching" of students so that they all use the terms in a similar way.

COACHING DEFINITIONS

Academic Coaching involves students practicing intellectual skills while teachers facilitate that practice: correcting bad habits, asking evocative questions and helping students measure their progress. Classroom coaching is analogous to musical or athletic coaching whereby students build positive performance habits through intense practice. As such, intellectual coaching should occupy 60 to 80% of instructional time in most Paideia classrooms. Ultimately, academic coaching becomes much more powerful and relevant when students and teachers collaborate on a formal, product-oriented classroom project.

The *Coached Project* is most like a traditional unit of classroom study in that it is often two to three weeks in duration and thematically integrated. Whenever possible, coached projects involve several disciplines and engage multiple intelligences. Often, they provide the context for practicing a number of different intellectual skills. The project itself is analogous to the period of rehearsal and practice that precedes a recital or game. They are different from more traditional units of study in that students are often very involved in planning the project and assessing common progress toward a product of real-world value.

The *Product* toward which students and teacher are working in a coached project often has an audience and, in part because of this audience, the product has value in the world outside the classroom. Because of this real-world audience, students become vested in producing a quality product and so accept high standards for the academic work involved in producing the product. The product is analogous to the concert or playoff game that comes at the end of a period of intense practice and preparation. It is what gives the entire project—and the academic work it contains—relevance for the students doing the work.

PRODUCTS AND PERFORMANCES IN CONTEXT

Teachers often find this worksheet useful when planning projects and even use it with groups of students to enlist and focus student input in project planning. It becomes all the more useful when teachers use the Purpose column to list the appropriate knowledge and skills that the project should encompass. You should use this sheet to align the project's parts with any standard curriculum for which you and your students are responsible.

STUDENT PRODUCT(S)/PERFORMANCES

PRODUCT/ PERFORMANCE	PURPOSE	AUDIENCE	WAY OF SHARING	CRITERIA FOR ASSESSING

A MODEL OF INTELLECTUAL SKILLS

This simple model of intellectual skills serves to remind us of the variety of thinking skills involved in mastering most subjects. Within the context of our coached projects, we need to encourage students to expand the range of their thinking (thus the variety of types listed here) as well as the depth (thus the more complex models are listed separately). One productive use of this or a similar model is as a checklist that can be applied to student project work to measure just how comprehensive is the intellectual input required to produce a given product.

Basic Thinking Processes

CAUSATION—establishing cause and effect; assessment
    Predictions
    Inferences
    Judgments
    Evaluations

TRANSFORMATIONS—relating known to unknown characteristics; creating meanings
    Analogies
    Metaphors
    Logical inductions

CLASSIFICATION—determining common qualities
    Similarities and differences
    Grouping and sorting; comparisons
    Either/or distinctions

QUALIFICATIONS—finding unique characteristics
    Units of basic identity
    Definitions; facts
    Problem/task recognition

Complex Thinking Processes

PROBLEM SOLVING—resolve a known difficulty
  Transformations
  Causation
  —Solutions; generalizations

DECISION MAKING—choose a best alternative
  Classifications
  Relationships
  —Responses

CRITICAL THINKING—understand particular meanings
  Relationships
  Transformations
  Causation
  —Sound reasons; proofs; theories

CREATIVE THINKING—create novel or aesthetic
ideas/products
  Qualifications
  Relationships
  Transformations
  —New meanings; products

THREE-COLUMN LESSON PLANS

What follows on pages 115–121 is the lesson plan for a two-week coached project that integrates all three columns of instruction. It was developed by second grade teachers at Madison Elementary School in Guilford County, North Carolina, and is based on a similar project from the Pueblo School of Arts and Sciences, a Paideia Charter School in Pueblo, Colorado. The final product is a glow-in-the-dark ocean, an educational environment that second-grade students share with kindergarten and first-grade students in their school.

Following the elementary lesson plan is a coached project, pages 122–123, for eleventh grade language arts: a three-column lesson plan for a reader's theater production of Thomas Wolfe's short story, "The Lost Boy." This unit was developed to teach both the American short story and, more specifically, narrative styles and points of view. The four sections of the story are each told from a radically different point of view and each is set in a radically different time period—even though each involves the same characters. The teacher originally divided her class into four production groups to write a reader's theater script for each section and to prepare their part of the whole production. Through seminar discussion of the story and in postproduction written assignments, the class was able to establish a much more sophisticated understanding of narrative points of view.

These and similar lesson plans are instructive because they stress how all three columns combine into one powerful cycle of instruction.

GLOW-IN-THE-DARK OCEAN LESSON PLAN

Grade Level: 2nd   Theme: Relationships   Students produce art
Unit: Oceans   Product: Glow-in-the-   projects during guid-
                    Dark Ocean (Presenta-   ed reading and whole
                    tion for K & 1)   group for the "Glow-
                                            in-the-Dark Ocean"
                                            presentation

                                            Date: May 19–May 30

DIDACTIC	COACHING	SEMINARS
Week 1		
Monday: 1. Read aloud 1 of these:	2. "What is an Ocean?" Read pp. 154–159 in *Discover Science* with a partner. Write a para-graph about what you learned.	
The Great White Man-eating Shark *The Wishing Fish* *I Wonder if I'll See a Whale* *Alistair Underwater*		
3. Shared Writ-ing—Teacher writes what stu-dents learned on a chart as they share with the class.	4. Literature Workstations	
5. Science Activity (Evaporation of Salt Water)—p. 158 in *Discover Science*	6. Work with a part-ner to write a hypothesis.	
7. Introduce graphic organizer from *Windows on Sci-ence Vol. 2, Surface Features* p. 176.	8. Students work in groups to com-plete graphic organizer.	
Show laserdisc: TE pp. 151–155.		

DIDACTIC	COACHING	SEMINARS
	Tuesday 1. Work in groups of 3. Read "The Silver Bay" in *Front Row*. Using story paper, retell the story. Illustrate. Use aluminum foil for the sea gull or the bay.	
3. Teacher models cursive writing on overhead. Poem p. 280 in *Make a Splash*.	2. Literature Workstations/Guided Reading Guided Reading: *Brown Bear, Brown Bear*. Children read in small group. Make a book. "Sea gull, sea gull, what do you see?" "Otter Side of the Story" (article). Children read in small groups. Make an octopus wind sock with Fruit Loops for suction cups.	
6. Math 7.9 Teacher models repeated addition using Pepperidge Farm Goldfish. Write a # sentence and model.	4. Students practice cursive. 5. Make a word. Teacher scrambles letters for "oceanography" on the board. Students work together to see how many words they can make. Can they	

DIDACTIC	COACHING	SEMINARS
8. Writing Read "Sea Shore Story" p. 147 in *Front Row.*	use all the letters to find the bonus word? 7. Students use goldfish and construction paper to model repeated addition. 9. Work with partner to write a story about living under the sea. Teacher edits as students finish. Students publish their stories on chart paper.	
Wednesday 1. Read aloud *Kermit the Hermit* 4. Groups share their sequencing. Class judges. Class choice sequences their story on sentence strips. 6. Math—Points on a grid 6.4. Review points on a grid and coordinates.	Wednesday 2. Students work in groups to sequence the story. 3. Workstations/Guided Reading Guided Reading: Read *Swimmy* in *Window to the Sky.* Sponge paint bulletin board with glow-in-the-dark paint. Use paper plates to make fish. Color with glow-in-the-dark crayons. 5. Spelling—Work with a partner. Practice the words we make	

DIDACTIC	COACHING	SEMINARS
	from oceanography on a slate.	
	7. Play "Hide Your Treasure"	
	8. Writing—Continue working on stores from Tuesday.	
Thursday	Thursday	Thursday
3. Handwriting—Teacher models poem "On Our Bikes," p. 154 in *Front Row*.	2. Workstations/ Guided Reading Guided Reading: *Henry's Wrong Turn.*	1. *Kermit the Hermit*
5. Math 2.2 Symmetry Review Symmetry	Color paper with glow-in-the-dark crayons. Make origami whales.	
7. Review *Kermit the Hermit*	4. Students practice cursive and spelling words.	
	6. Students work together to complete "Ocean Symmetry."	
	8. Work with a partner to write a story about what you would give to repay someone for saving your life.	
Friday FIELD DAY		

DIDACTIC	COACHING	SEMINARS
Week 2		
Monday		
1. Laser Disc— "Ocean Life," pp. 160–164; "Oceans Depth," pp. 166–169.	2. Students work together to write a paragraph about what they learned.	
4. Watch *Reading Rainbow: Jack, the Seal and the Sea*. Discuss conservation and pollution.	3. Workstations/ Guided Reading Guided Reading: "A Monster of the Sea" in *Young America*. Do crayon resist art project. Be sure to include plants. Use glow-in-the-dark crayons.	
6. Make a class wave bottle.		
7. Read aloud— "The World Ocean" (article)	5. Students read pp. 171–173 from *Windows on Science* with a partner. Work together to write a paragraph about what they learned.	
	8. Students work together to produce "Save Our Oceans" posters.	
Tuesday	**Tuesday**	
1. Read aloud *The Rainbow Fish*	2. Students retell story on story paper. Illustrate. Use aluminum foil.	
4. Watch *Humphrey the Lost Whale* (T49)		

DIDACTIC	COACHING	SEMINARS
5. Math—Money Review counting coins.	3. Workstations/ Guided Reading Guided Reading: *How to Hide* and *Octopus & Creatures of the Sea.* Make camouflage fish pictures using glow-in-the-dark crayons. Workstations: Everybody does "Hide and Seek Booklet." 6. Students work together to solve "Ocean Money." 7. Writing—Make cards for Reading Buddies.	
Wednesday 1. Read aloud—*Sea Creatures Do Amazing Things,* pp. 64–69. Make jelly fish using ziplock sandwich bags filled with light tissue paper. Use white crepe paper for tentacles. 4. Watch *Reading Rainbow—Dive to the Coral Reef* (T49).	Wednesday 2. Workstations/ Guided Reading Guided Reading: "Super Shark" (article). Make sharks out of large construction paper. Color with glow-in-the-dark crayons. 3. Students work together to read and complete the Scholastic News about coral reefs.	

DIDACTIC	COACHING	SEMINARS
6. Teacher models "Coral Creations."	5. Math—Graphs/ Problem Solving Students work together to complete "Animals at Seaside Park." 7. Students invent their own coral creation.	
Thursday 4. Math—Place Value. Review place value.	Thursday 2. Workstations 3. FIELD TRIP WITH READING BUDDIES 5. Students complete "Alligator and the Fish." 6. Practice for presentation!	Thursday 1. *The Rainbow Fish*

NARRATIVE STYLES IN FICTION LESSON PLAN

Unit/Topic: <u>Narrative Styles in Fiction</u>

Length of Project: <u>12 days</u>

Curriculum Objectives: <u>Short story, narrative styles, points of view</u>

Grade: <u>11th Grade English</u>

Product/Performance: <u>Readers' Theatre: "The Lost Boy"</u>

DIDACTIC	COACHING	SEMINARS
Day One: 　Didactic Presentation 　a. Narrative persona 　b. Points of view 　c. Examples 　d. Readers' theatre as a production	*Day Two:* 　a. Facilitated Discussion of Project/Product 　b. Division of class into four production teams (1, 2, 3, 4) *Day Three:* 　a. Facilitated Discussion of the four story sections as different types of narrative 　b. Division within production teams into work groups	
Day Four: 　Didactic Presentation: Thomas Wolfe and his family	*Day Four:* 　Work teams in production	
		Day Five: 　Seminar: Wolfe's "The Lost Boy"

Days Six and Seven:
 a. Script teams at
 work
 b. Stage set team
 in design
 c. Promotion
 teams meet
 together

Day Eight:
 a. Assign parts
 b. Read through
 draft script in
 four groups
 c. Script revision

Day Nine:
 a. Staged lighting
 setup
 b. Script revision

Day Ten:
 Dress rehearsal
 leading to:

Day Eleven:
 a. Three produc-
 tions, including
 evening perfor-
 mance for
 community
 b. Written reflec-
 tion on narrative
 points of view

Possible Seminar on
second Wolfe
short story to fol-
low unit and to
focus on "Point
of view."

APPENDIX C

ASSESSMENT INSTRUMENTS

There is no area in the Paideia classroom where teachers are more in need of specific tools than assessment. Teachers who have only recently been trained to use checklists, rubrics, and portfolios to measure and encourage student progress often request tools specifically tailored to the seminar and coached project. Although the tools included in Appendix C are useful, you shouldn't stop with these assessment instruments. As you become a more experienced seminar leader and coach, you should work with students to develop their own tools for the texts and projects that best deliver *their* curriculum.

PAIDEIA ASSESSMENT

Once a teacher has been trained in seminar leadership and project coaching, the next logical step is to focus on assessment as the culmination of the training process. In this Appendix (as in Chapter 5), we use the term *assessment* to mean the quality control work that teachers and students do in collaboration. In many ways, assessment is an integral part of the learning process because it forces students as well as teachers to be constantly aware of what knowledge and skills they have—and have not—mastered. In addition, collaborative assessment may well be the key to building a trusting and respectful relationship between teacher and students.

The simplest form of assessment tool is a checklist, a list of positive behaviors that either are or are not exhibited during a learning event. This simple seminar checklist is one of a number of examples that teachers and students have developed to remind them of effective learning behaviors.

SEMINAR RATING CHART

for _____

date_____

Positive Behaviors

__ 1. I came prepared for seminar.

__ 2. I was courteous to the other students.

__ 3. I paused and thought before speaking.

__ 4. I listened to others tell their ideas.

__ 5. I kept an open mind for opinions different from my own.

__ 6. I acted as a positive role model for other students.

__ 7. I built on what was just said before I gave my own opinion.

__ 8. I used fixed examples from the text to back up statements.

__ 9. I felt comfortable speaking in seminar.

__ 10. I gave my opinions clearly.

Negative Behaviors

__ 11. I interrupted others.

__ 12. I acted silly.

__ 13. I did not look at the person speaking.

__ 14. I talked off topic.

__ 15. I talked too much or not at all.

A CHECKLIST GRID

To measure and communicate clearly about the growth in a student's skills, teachers often use a chronological grid that reflects that student's behavior in a series of seminars. This example is divided into four relatively generic sections (conduct, speaking/reasoning, listening, and reading), and the teacher is to fill in specific checklist items in the left-hand column. The actual seminar texts and dates are recorded across the top of the grid, and the student and teacher collaborate on "checking off" each seminar performance in turn.

Simple grids such as this can be an effective part of a student's seminar portfolio because the grids graphically summarize the student's progress as a participant, serving to remind, at a glance, both teacher and student which skills a student needs to focus on in upcoming seminars.

CHECKLIST GRID OF PAIDEIA SEMINAR BEHAVIORS

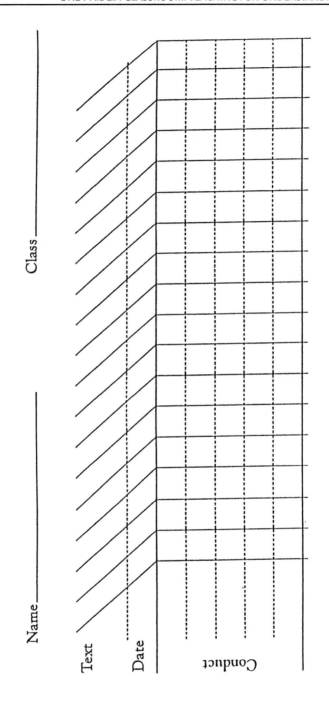

Name _____

Class _____

Text

Date

Conduct

Speaking/Reasoning						Listening					Reading			

SEMINAR RUBRICS I

The next stage in sophistication after a checklist of seminar skills is a seminar rubric that allows students and teachers to judge and record several levels of mastery of a specific skill. The following example is an elementary seminar rubric. The skills listed in this case are not unlike those of a checklist, but here a student is assessed according to how often the student exhibits each behavior on a scale of 1–5:

1 = not yet
2 = occasionally
3 = often
4 = frequently
5 = always.

Note that a grid such as the previous one could be used to record the results of such a rubric, graphically recording a student's progress over time.

PAIDEIA SEMINAR RUBRIC

CONDUCT	LISTENING
Student sits seminar style.	Student looks at person who is speaking.
Student looks at person talking and listens to learn.	Student asks questions about what has been said.
Student waits for turn to speak.	Student talks about what he or she has heard.
Student is polite.	
1 2 3 4 5	1 2 3 4 5
SPEAKING	CRITICAL THINKING
Student speaks clearly with appropriate voice level.	The student's response reflects listening to the text and going beyond the text.
Student expresses complete thoughts.	The student's response reflects listening to others.
Student's comments relate to the text, questions, or previous statements.	Student can explain why he or she disagrees with another student and can support it from the text.
Student's comments show respect for self and others.	Student response reflects comprehension of text; answers are thought out.
Students ask questions.	Student makes statements that indicate application to real world situations.
1 2 3 4 5	1 2 3 4 5

1=not yet   2=occasionally   3=often   4=frequently   5=always

SEMINAR RUBRICS II

This example was created at the Chattanooga School of Arts and Sciences for use in secondary seminars. Using this rubric, a student can score 1 to 4 points in each of five areas. A student may receive a high score in one area but a lower score in another area.

In contrast to the rubric on the previous page, this example offers detailed descriptions of each skill level, which makes it more abstract yet more comprehensive. This rubric was developed by teachers and students working together, something we recommend because the process of writing the rubric descriptions can be educational for students as well as teachers.

(The Chattanooga Rubric is on pages 136–139.)

ASSESSING PERFORMANCE IN A SOCRATIC SEMINAR

CONDUCT	LEADERSHIP	REASONING	LISTENING	READING
Demonstrates respect, enthusiasm and skill for the purpose of seminar; insight into important texts and ideas gained through the interplay of collaborative and personal inquiry. Demonstrates in speech and manner a habitual respect for processes and norms of reasoned discussion and shared inquiry. Effectively contributes to deepen & broaden the conversation, revealing exemplary habits of mind.	Takes clear responsibility for the seminar's progress or lack of it. Takes stock of overall direction and effectiveness of the discussion, and takes apt steps to refocus or redirect conversation and/or to cause others to rethink previous statements. Offers apt feedback and effective guidance to others. Takes steps to involve reticent participants and to insure that unnoticed points are attended to.	Arguments are so reasonable, apt, logical, and substantial with evidence from the text as to consistently move the conversation forward and deepen the inquiry effectively. The analyses made are helpful in clarifying complex ideas. Criticisms made are never ad hominem.	Listens unusually well. Takes steps routinely to comprehend what is said, is consistently attentive (as reflected in direct and indirect evidence), and later responses (actions, comments, and writings) indicate accurate and perceptive listening.	Conduct and written work indicate student has read the text carefully, is thoroughly familiar with the text and its main ideas. Can offer insightful interpretations and evaluations of it, is respectful of the text while also reading it critically, and has come prepared with thoughtful questions and reaction.

Score = 4

CONDUCT	LEADERSHIP	REASONING	LISTENING	READING
Demonstrates in speech and manner an overall respect for and understanding of the goals, processes, and norms of reasoned discussion and shared inquiry. Participates to advance conversation and displays mature habits of mind, but may be sometimes ineffective in sharing inquiry or working with others.	Is generally willing to take on facilitative roles and responsibilities. *Either* makes regular efforts to be helpful (in moving the conversation forward and/or including others in it) but is sometimes ineffective in doing so, *or* does not typically take a leadership role but is effective when does so.	Arguments are generally reasonable, apt, and logical. There may be some minor flaws in reasoning, evidence, or aptness of remarks, but the ideas contribute to an understanding of the text or comments made by others.	Listens well. Takes steps to comprehend what is said. Generally pays attention and/or responds appropriately to ideas and questions by other participants.	Conduct and written work generally indicate that student has read the text carefully, can offer reasonable, if sometimes incomplete or questionable, interpretations, and has come with apt questions and ideas regarding it.

Score = 3

CONDUCT	LEADERSHIP	REASONING	LISTENING	READING
Speech and manner suggest that the student misunderstands the purpose of the discussion and/or is undisciplined concerning seminar practices and necessary habits of mind. May contribute, even frequently, to the conversation, but is somewhat ineffective due to opinionated or unclear and undeveloped views.	Takes on facilitative roles and responsibilities infrequently and/or ineffectively. When taking on a leadership role, may misconstrue the responsibility by lobbying for favored opinions or speakers only and/or by trying to close discussion prematurely.	Unsubstantial or undeveloped opinions offered more often than sound arguments. Comments suggest student has some difficulty in moving beyond mere reaction to thorough arguments, or difficulty in following complex arguments of others (as reflected in questions asked and/or non sequiturs). Student may resort to ad hominem attacks instead of focusing on the critique of claims and arguments.	Does not regularly listen very well and/or is not always attentive, as reflected in comments and body language. Verbal reactions tend to reflect an earlier failure to listen carefully to what was said.	Comments indicate that student may have read the text but has misunderstood the text and/or read the text from a too present-centered stance and/or has not put enough focused effort into seminar preparation. Or, varying conduct and written work indicate that the student's preparation is inconsistent.

Score = 2

Score = 1

CONDUCT	LEADERSHIP	REASONING	LISTENING	READING
Speech and manner display little respect for or understanding of the seminar process. Student appears to lack essential habits of mind. Student is either routinely argumentative, distracting, and/or obstinate or student is disengaged—extremely reluctant to participate, even when called on (to the point of making others feel the detachment).	Plays no active facilitation role of any kind or actions are consistently counter-productive in that role.	Comments suggest student has great difficultly with analytical requirements of seminar. Remarks routinely appear to be non sequiturs and/or illogical or without substantiation and not followable by others, and/or student may resort to ad hominem comments about text author.	Does not listen adequately, as reflected in later questions or comments (e.g., non sequiturs and repetition of earlier points as if they hadn't been spoken) and/or body language very suggestive of inattentiveness.	Student is *either* generally unable to make adequate meaning of text *or* generally comes to class unprepared.

POSTSEMINAR REFLECTION

What follows is a set of suggested questions teachers and students can ask collaboratively as part of a postseminar reflection exercise. Note that our emphasis here is on both seminar process and content; we hope that the teacher will ask students to reflect privately in writing as well as publicly in discussion on both aspects of the seminar.

Teachers who use these guidelines are often careful to vary the questions they ask from seminar to seminar depending on the quality and tenor of each discussion. See Chapter 5 for an example of a postseminar exercise that capitalizes on the educational riches produced by the seminar itself.

SEMINAR REFLECTION QUESTIONS

The goal is to assess the seminar in terms of both process and content—individually and collectively.

Individual, private, *written* assessment is coupled with collective, public, *oral* assessment.

Preseminar:

1. What did you have to do to prepare for this seminar?
2. Did you have previous knowledge about this text?
3. What did you expect from this seminar?

Seminar:

1. How did your participation affect the seminar? The group process?
2. How did the group handle the task of analyzing and evaluating the text?
3. What ideas became more important to you throughout the seminar?
4. How did the participants treat each other?
5. What influence did the facilitator have?

Postseminar:

1. Was there anything about the seminar that bothered you?
2. Was the text appropriate and challenging? Why/why not?
3. What will you remember about the seminar?
4. What suggestions would you make to improve the seminar?
5. What do you/we need to work on next time?

ASSESSING AN INDIVIDUAL SEMINAR

Amy Bender's "Seminar Teaching Guide" is a comprehensive checklist to be used to assess an individual seminar, not for evaluating the performance of an individual teacher or student. It was developed as part of Bender's dissertation research in 1995. She developed the checklist through several drafts based on the suggestions and revisions of a number of experienced seminar leaders. It is an excellent reminder of the number and variety of elements that contribute to quality seminars.

Many teachers use this checklist for self- or peer-assessment and periodically review seminars they have led so that they can document and study their progress in a teacher portfolio. It is used here with the permission of Amy Bender, PhD.

SEMINAR TEACHING GUIDE

This instrument can be used by teachers for self-assessment, by administrators and other colleagues to determine teacher effectiveness, and by trainers when instructing new learners. It is designed to provide information and guidance in areas that can be improved, and the observer using the instrument should provide suggestions to the teacher for improvement. The seminar leader can be videotaped conducting a seminar, and then following the seminar the individual can view the video alone or with another colleague using the instrument to determine areas that could be improved in his or her seminar leading. Part 1 of the instrument is a checklist with space left between the items for specific comments about those items. The teacher can use that space to explain why a behavior occurred or did not occur, and in that space the observer can note suggestions for improvement or provide examples of the behavior that occurred. Part 2 is a short answer portion that can be filled in by the teacher before self-evaluation or talking with an administrator or another colleague.

In some cases, the items will contain an AND. The observer should be aware of this and note that mastering one portion of the item does not necessarily mean that item has been satisfactorily completed. The observer should write in the space provided explaining which parts of the item were done satisfactorily and which were not.

As you complete the instrument, please remember that the purpose of the *Seminar Teaching Guide* is to provide guidance and feedback (not only from other individuals but also for self-assessment) on the conduct of the seminar. The instrument is a profile with suggestions for improvement, and it is not designed to yield a score that could be used to rank or rate the performance of the teacher. All of the items are not equally important and a ranking would not be beneficial.

Training is necessary before using the instrument to provide specific, helpful recommendations to teachers and to make sure the items are interpreted as intended.

The teacher should attach a copy of the questions prepared for use during the seminar.

Name _____

Grade Level _____

Subject _____

Part 1
Preparation for Seminar

	Yes	No
1. Text chosen was appropriate for a seminar AND the age of the students.	___	___
2. The room was set up so that participants could make eye contact with each other (e.g., circle or square).	___	___
3. Teacher had clearly stated expectations for behavior as evidenced by the students' actions.	___	___

Teacher as Facilitator

4. Teacher was seated on the same level as the students with them in the seminar.	___	___
5. Teacher was knowledgeable about the text being discussed AND could locate references in the text quickly.	___	___
6. Teacher refrained from giving his or her own opinion during the seminar.	___	___

	Yes	No

7. Teacher encouraged student interaction (listening as well as speaking) by keeping track of those who spoke, providing opportunities for shy students, asking follow-up questions, AND asking students to respond to what had been said.

8. Teacher guided students when they made factual errors by further questioning or probing if they were not corrected by other students.

9. Teacher asked for clarification AND connections between ideas.

10. Teacher brought students back to the text when digressing.

11. Teacher kept one or two students from dominating or monopolizing the conversation.

12. Teacher kept the seminar participants from arguing out of control.

13. Teacher occasionally paraphrased students' remarks when necessary.

14. Teacher stopped misbehavior quickly AND effectively if students made no effort to curb each others' inappropriate behavior.

15. Teacher accepted, encouraged, AND supported divergent views and opinions.

	Yes	No

16. Teacher included the whole group in the discussion AND did not focus on only a few members of the group.

17. Teacher's body language AND facial expressions were accepting of all students.

18. Teacher refrained from providing traditional closure for the students by summarizing at the end of the seminar.

Questioning Strategies

19. Opening question was broad AND each participant was given an opportunity to respond.

20. Teacher was a good listener AND framed follow-up questions from student comments.

21. Teacher asked questions that generated higher-order thinking (synthesis, analysis, or evaluation) responses from the students.

22. Teacher asked questions that encouraged students to explore relevance of text to their present lives.

23. Teacher allowed sufficient wait-time for students to think before the students responded or another question was asked.

24. Questions posed did not lead the students to a preconceived "right" answer.

	Yes	No

25. Teacher made smooth transitions between questions asked.

26. Teacher questioned students, not telling or teaching factual knowledge about the text.

Student Participation

27. Students had a copy of the text being discussed in front of them.

28. Students observed the rules of seminar participation (put chairs in circle, expectations of behavior for teacher and student).

29. Students talked more than the teacher.

30. Students did not require permission (from the teacher or other students) to speak during the seminar.

31. Students their directed comments to each other rather than the teacher.

32. Students showed respect for others' views and opinions by listening AND by not criticizing other students for differing responses.

33. Students supported their statements with references to the text.

	Yes	**No**
34. Students used each others' names when agreeing or disagreeing with other students.	____	____
35. Students asked questions during the seminar.	____	____
36. Students were comfortable sharing opinions based on text evidenced by a conversation-like atmosphere.	____	____

Part 2

This portion of the instrument is designed to give the teacher an opportunity to reflect on the seminar and to provide additional information to the observer that may make a difference in the observation. Please answer the following questions as specifically as possible at the bottom of the page or attach additional pages to the end of this instrument.

I have led _____ (approximate number) seminars this year with this class.

Were you comfortable leading this seminar? Are there any special circumstances that should be considered by a person observing who has not been in your class every day?

How does this seminar text fit into your lesson plans?

What did you do to prepare the students for the seminar (pre-seminar activities, coaching, or didactic instruction)?

What kind of follow-up activities are planned for the students?

How do you determine student understanding of the seminar?

After completing this observation, what areas of your seminar leading do you feel need improvement?

STUDENT PROJECT RUBRIC

Unlike the previous checklist, this assessment tool can be used to establish the quality of an individual student's work over the course of a generic coached project. Because coached projects are so different in scope and content, teachers may want to work with students to either revise existing rubrics or create new rubrics tailored to specific projects, so that the assessment process can contribute as much as possible to the learning process.

(The Student Project Rubric is found on pages 152–153.)

STUDENT PROJECT RUBRIC

	Understanding of Topic/Task	Quality of Plan/Procedures
0	**Not Understood** Student cannot discuss project task.	**Inadequate** Student's plan doesn't meet project criteria.
1	**Fairly Understood** Student repeats task as defined in project description.	**Adequate** Student's plan meets basic project criteria.
2	**Understood** Student rephrases project description in own words.	**Refined** Student's approach reflects a personalized approach to meeting project criteria.
3	**Generalized, Applied, Extended** Student rephrases project description in own words and can describe objectives of project relative to outcomes.	**Sophisticated** Student's plan reflects a personalized approach to meeting project criteria and clearly illustrates reasoning for decisions.

Quality of Presentation	Demonstration of Knowledge
Lacking Effort Student is disorganized, does not participate in discussion.	**Substandard** Student cannot answer questions about content of project.
Minimal Effort Student presents work to date, relies on Committee to lead discussion.	**Basic** Student answers questions about basic content of project.
Proficient, Complete Student presents work to date in orderly fashion, offers information about projects/process to Committee.	**Standard** Student answers questions about content of project and can relate information to similar issues.
Well-Organized, Detailed, Creative Student presents work to date in orderly, clearly prepared fashion, leads discussion about projects/process with Committee.	**Proficient** Student answers questions about content of project, can relate information to similar issues, and apply basic concepts to more complex issues.

PAIDEIA TEACHER PORTFOLIO

In addition to the more obvious uses for student portfolios in the Paideia classroom, many teachers are now using a Paideia Teacher Portfolio to document their growth as:

◆ Seminar leaders,

◆ Coaches of product-oriented projects,

◆ Experts on collaborative assessment, or

◆ All of the above.

In addition, many administrators in Paideia schools are using (if not actually requiring) this sort of documentation to encourage and judge professional growth.

A portfolio is most powerful as a reflective tool that teachers use to learn from experience and so better prepare for future teaching. As such, it should include their own teaching journal notes as well as student input.

PAIDEIA TEACHER PORTFOLIO

Suggested Contents:

- Seminar Texts
- Seminar Notes and Questions
- Preseminar Activities
- Seminar Map
- Postseminar Activity
- Facilitator Checklist

- Coached Project Plans
- Coached Project Notes
- Coached Project Checklists
- Coached Project Products

- Assessment Tools Used for Seminars and Coached Projects
- Student Evaluations of Teacher Performance
- Reflective Journal Notes

BIBLIOGRAPHY

Adler, Mortimer J. *Paideia Problems and Possibilities.* New York: MacMillan, 1983.

Adler, Mortimer J. *The Paideia Program.* New York: MacMillan, 1984.

Adler, Mortimer J. *The Paideia Proposal.* New York: MacMillan, 1982.

Chesser, William, Gail Gellatly, and Michael Hale. (1997, Sept.). "Do Paideia seminars explain higher writing scores?" *Middle School Journal,* 40–44.

Gardner, Howard. *Frames of Mind: The Theory of Multiple Intelligences.* New York: Basic Books, 1993.

Herman, R. and Sam Stringfield. *Ten Promising Programs for Educating Disadvantaged Students.* Baltimore: Johns Hopkins, 1995.

Hirsch, Robert Maynard. *Cultural Literacy: What Every American Needs to Know.* New York: Vintage Books, 1988.

Hutchins, R. M. *The Great Conversation. Vol. 1 of Great Books of the Western World.* Chicago: Encyclopedia Britannica, 1952.

Nesselrodt, P. and E. Schaffer. (1995, June). "Early Findings from Study of the Paideia Program's Effects." *Paideia Next Century,* p. 1.

Roberts, Terry, and the Staff of the National Paideia Center. *The Power of Paideia Schools: Defining Lives Through Learning.* Alexandria, VA: ASCD, 1998.

The Secretary's Commission on Achieving Necessary Skills. (1991). *What Work Requires of Schools: A SCANS Report for America 2000.* Washington, DC: U.S. Department of Labor.